COMMENTS ON WORK ~~ ~~

Listen America, You Don't Even Ow has gained notoriety for successf distribution network and selling his l notoriety for the content of his boc American Mavericks which began q~~..~~, ~~..~~ ~~.....~~au and grew louder with Henry Miller, Kerouac, and Bukowski." Miles Moore, poet, critic.

When Cuba Was a Virgin, memoir: "Your book is probably too macho for today's editors, so many of whom are women. This is a man's book and women may not like it." Jeffrey Simmons, literary agent, London.

When Cuba Was a Virgin: "When I was an assistant editor, I spent a healthy amount of time going through the slush pile and was amazed to find in its depths a work of such originality, verve, and dexterity as Joyce's memoir of his time in Cuba." David Adams, editor, MacAdam/Cage publishers, San Francisco. Adams was fired two weeks after he wrote this letter.

First Born of an Ass, novel: "Believe me, I wish I had had the sense, or perception, or instinct, to publish *First Born of an Ass* when it was submitted here." Robert Loomis, Vice-President, Random House, NYC.

The Recorder of Births & Deaths, short stories: "An astounding work of contemporary absurdist literature." Mary Banas, reviewer, *Booklist*.

First Born of an Ass: "Yes, the printing of your novel is going to be delayed again. The man who was doing the typesetting is a Mennonite and when he came to the part where your hero's turds start talking, he freaked out. He ran from the room, screaming, 'the devil's in this book, the devil's in this book.' So now we have to look for a new typesetter." Gaylord Dold, editor, Watermark Books.

"Like any other true original – it is not out of place to mention Miller and Lawrence – Joyce has had a hard time getting his work appreciated. And Joyce is, at least to the unadventurous, an unplaceable writer. He sets his own standards, writes according to his own unique vision. He is the sort of writer whom, years later, editors will be using to set criteria by." John Oakes, publisher, Avalon Conglomerate.

HOW CENSORSHIP OPERATES IN THE UNITED STATES

Jack Shafer (editor of *City Paper*, Wash. D.C., who first published essays on Miller, Bukowski, & Stettner): "All my friends have advised me I'd be better off severing my ties with you." Shafer, now at Slate.com, continued to publish the author's essays.

Jack Garlington, editor of *Western Humanities Review* (University of Utah), 1970–1981: "We are happy to accept your poem *In This World of Terror & Pig-Headed Conmen* for the winter 1975 issue." Shortly after the poem (10 pages) appeared, Garlington was called into an office by the university's administrators and told he would be fired on grounds of "moral turpitude" if he published any more of William Joyce's writings. Garlington complied, until the month before his retirement.

Alice Fulton, poet, University of Michigan, (her book given negative review by the author) to David Levine, one of her students, and a former researcher for the author: "Mr. Levine, I wasn't here this summer, but had I been here and seen William Joyce on your résumé, you not only would not have gotten a fellowship but you wouldn't have gotten into this university."

Lewis Lapham, former editor of *Harper's Magazine*, NYC, upon being asked by the author why his essay on U.S. writing hadn't appeared in a more conspicuous journal: "My friends told me that if I tried to publish this, I could put my career in a bottle and cast it in the wine-dark sea."

M.L. Hester, publisher, Avisson publishers, original U.S. publisher of *Miller, Bukowski & Their Enemies*: "I've gotten some emails advising me to discontinue your book." Hester did discontinue the book shortly thereafter though a year earlier he had advised the author, "Yours is one of the few books that tells the truth."

Washington Post Book Reviewer in conversation with the author: "Your novel (*First Born of an Ass*) certainly shows some talent but you have to understand we are a family newspaper."

MILLER, BUKOWSKI AND THEIR ENEMIES

Guillermo O'Joyce

pinter
&
martin

Miller, Bukowski & their enemies

This new edition with nine new essays first published
in Great Britain by Pinter & Martin Ltd 2011

ISBN 978-1-905177-27-1 (paperback)
ISBN 978-1-905177-98-1 (ebook)

British Library Cataloguing-in-Publication Data
A catalogue record for this book is available from the British Library

Printed in Great Britain by TJ International Ltd, Padstow, Cornwall

Pinter & Martin Ltd
6 Effra Parade
London SW2 1PS

www.pinterandmartin.com

contents

For Jack Shafer, the rare editor with balls

About Guillermo O'Joyce

The poems and stories of Guillermo O'Joyce have been appearing in magazine and books (under William Joyce) since 1968. He rides a styrofoam body board on the waves at Canoa, Ecuador and survives by playing poker and studying frigate birds. His novel *First Born of an Ass* has a talking turd in it. His poetry book *Listen America, You Don't Even Own Your Name* has a poem about the sexual history of the U.S.

Manuscripts-in-waiting include a comic memoir, *When Cuba Was a Virgin*, and *Unusual Places, Remarkable People*, travel stories. O'Joyce will be coming to Europe to do an extended tour of readings of Bukowski's poetry.

guillermojoyce@gmail.com

Acknowledgements

"Miller Time" first appeared in *City Paper* (Washington, D.C.) as an extended essay/review prompted by the book *The Happiest Man Alive: A Biography of Henry Miller*, by Mary V. Dearborn. "Kiss Me, I'm Still Alive" also first appeared in *City Paper*, as did "His Own Best Friend," prompted by the book *Hank: The Life of Charles Bukowski*, by Neeli Cherkovski.

"Masturbation in the Strophe Factory" is a compendium of four essays. The first, carrying that same title, appeared in *Cedar Rock*; the second, "The Present State of American Poetry II", in *New York Quarterly*; the third, "The Oink from the Literary Barn", in *American Book Review*; the fourth, "How Writers Censor Themselves", in *Yokoi*.

All other essays appear for the first time in this Pinter & Martin edition.

miller time: on henry miller

Henry Miller is not a writer; he's a friend you turn to when your apartment walls close in on you and all the world begins to stink. When you're most exasperated, Miller is there with his alternately cajoling, absurd, sincere, outraged, sage-like, funny voice, ruminating and gassing in a calm way. Miller's voice always comes from the quietest corner of the bar. The rest of the occupants are slaughtering each other, offering polemical speeches, toasting their various diseases, and gouging their own thighs and arms with their fingernails in an effort to rid themselves of the itch of being truly alive. Unlike his distant cousin Céline, Miller never gets clobbered by these barroom brawlers. He gets close enough to the action to observe the lice and the whispered endearments between blows, but he never gets whacked by a piece of flying furniture. "Don't struggle; get in the flow," he advises in book after book. Much of this "flow" for Miller is in the flotsam – all sorts of deranged and eccentric characters – who are both more lively and can tell us more about life than comfortable citizens at the center. He doesn't see the same divisions the rest of us have been taught to see. Wealthy hoarders or bourgeoisie hoarders may be deplorable, but the feeling I get after 30 years of browsing through Miller is that he'd knocked aside all compartmentalization; he would sit down for a meal with anybody who was unaffected and learn from him, provided of course that the companion sprung for the meal. Miller is the greatest of all freeloaders, surpassing even that other Joyce. In return for his presence, his attentive ear, and perhaps a three-page carbon of his latest writing, all Miller asks is that his host "would open all the windows leading to his heart" (about the Greek poet George Seferiades). And so people do. That is his secret – Miller was a great listener, though he has the reputation of a monologist.

He will rage, but he is never weighed down by alienation. He is a master of language, but literature doesn't mean a damn thing to him. I feel equally at home opening a Miller book on Page 7 or Page 57. It is like picking up the thread of a conversation I had five years ago with a trusty and trusting friend. The hermetically closed systems of the modern masters such as Joyce or Kafka mean little to him; they are only further evidence of The Machine that has reduced us all to atoms bouncing off our lonely apartment walls. Like Whitman, he advises us that all we have to do is open our arms and accept the world as it is. He echoes Thoreau in telling us to get off the conveyor belt and live simply. Yet, Miller has not an ounce of Whitman's optimism about the future of the United States, and his frenetic search for money and an audience kept him on the conveyor belt more than he would like us to believe. But it is that voice of his we always come back to. Even when I realize Miller has made a wrong turn, I stick with him. I do this because Miller takes the freedom to say anything that is on his mind at any given time. There is no holding back; he never falls for the echo of his rhetoric as many other good writers do. He is a singer for sure, but it is not his melody he becomes enraptured by, only the desire to be faithful to what he has seen and felt in his heart. If this seems a small order, listen to Chekhov: "I cannot remember a single new book in which the author does not do his best from the very first line to entangle himself in all sorts of conventionalities and compromise with his conscience. Deliberateness, cautiousness, craftiness but no freedom, no courage to write as one likes, and therefore no creative art." This remark covers most of the writing of our time, as it did in Europe in the late 19th century.

Most writers are attracted to craft because it's a chance to be evasive while romanticizing themselves. Even as most lawyers come to law not to serve justice, but to cut the pie of a legally sanctioned swindle, and as teachers come to the classroom to yak non-stop, thereby advancing the cause of impotency. Part of the definition of "human being" would include the unique ability to choose the vocation for which he is least suited.

Miller had risk, he had it in abundance. This was not a matter of using shocking sexual detail, as he was often accused of. It was a huge need to make his voice grow flesh. In the first 39 years of his life, before he fully committed himself to writing, Miller felt that everything we call "progress" was separating us from ourselves as well as each other. The "literary" voice was cut off from the body, and to eliminate the body was to eliminate the soul as well. Every new building, every new invention went a step further toward slicing people into strips of potato falling from the shredder. To reconnect himself, Miller felt he had to start from scratch, disconnect all the plugs that supposedly gave him sustenance but in reality sought to make him a galley slave and slowly inch himself back to being a whole person. To read Miller then is to listen to the first and last man on earth. Words aren't tools of the craft for him, as they are for most writers. Miller was as suspicious of them as he was of books. No, words were blasted from his liver and spleen and funny bone; they came rushing in measured torrents with lymph nodes and chunks of flesh stuck to them. There are considerable lumps in each of Miller's books where he goes off the deep end and makes no sense at all. This usually happens when he can't resist playing the new messiah and metaphysical poet wherein he trots out the stars and our relationship to the black holes in between. But always with Miller, I feel I am dealing with a man, not a code of conduct some publisher has put his stamp of approval on.

Of course there are other writers tapping away under a black firmament as if no one had ever thought to buy a typewriter before. Beckett comes to mind, with his heroes playing with their bedsores, mumbling asides to a mother who isn't there, their only company the bedpans and a few strands of aborted consciousness. Kafka is another, whispering from behind a closet door which in turn leads to another closet door that finally opens on the MLA (Modern Language Association) convention in Toledo, Ohio, where K, Lucky, and Malone enter to modest applause and the pedants rise to chant, "Oh Blessed Depression, Oh Blessed Symbols." It's gotten so bad that applicants for graduate-school English departments as far away as Cameroon have to write an essay on "How My Alienation Rendered Me Comatose." Pluckier souls are relegated to teaching remedial composition and running out for cheap sherry when the visiting poet comes to town.

It is true that only the courageous ones with unique voices offer themselves up for parody (is it possible to parody Saul "Give Me an Intellectual Smooch" Bellow or John "Count the Whorls in the Bannister" Updike?), but Miller took several important steps beyond what is called "modern literature."

First, Miller said there was no reason to despair. We ought to welcome breakdown, because the moral underpinnings of society indicate no morality at all but merely a devotion to ball bearings and cotter pins. If the legacy of the 20th century is war after war, chaos, corruption, incompetence, a will toward accumulating tidy comforts, the slaughter of everything vulnerable, root it on, says Miller. Let the whole cardboard house filled with pus collapse and ooze into the streets. "Suddenly inspired by the absolute hopelessness of everything, I felt relieved, felt as though a great burden had been lifted from my shoulders," he says in *Tropic of Cancer*. As to what Miller offers to replace cars, phones, soda pop, aspirin bottles, plastic drawings, and "enriched" bread, let him speak from a Greek island in 1939. He has no money, though he has published three books, no prospects, no home or homeland:

"I would set out in the morning and look for new coves and inlets to which to swim. There was never a soul about; I was like Robinson Crusoe on the island of Tobago. For hours at a stretch I would lie in the sun doing nothing, thinking nothing. To keep the mind empty is a feat, a very healthful feat too. To be silent the whole day long, see no newspaper, hear no radio, listen to no gossip, be thoroughly and completely lazy, thoroughly and completely indifferent to the fate of the world is the finest medicine a man can give himself. The booklearning gradually dribbles away; the problems melt and dissolve; ties are gently severed; thinking, when you deign to indulge in it, becomes very primitive; the body becomes a new and wonderful instrument; you look at plants or stones with different eyes; you wonder what people are struggling to accomplish by their frenetic activities. . . ."

Henry Miller understood it was rare to meet a man or woman who was at home on this earth. So he sought to show them the way by example and word. In a 1952 letter to Edmund Wilson, he explained that there was only one hero in his books – himself. If Miller carries the most gargantuan of egos, he also shows us how he made a mess of his life before he left for Paris in 1930. More important, he understands we are all feeling the same pressure, the same remoteness from our toes and genitals, trees and rivers, birds and other people. Yet, not only does Miller not feel alienated from other people, he assumes the world wants to hear him. This is a huge leap of faith when you consider that most people didn't want to hear him, that few publishers or agents would deal with him, that much of his best writing was banned in this country and most of Europe for 25 years, that he was so poor most of his life that he regularly had Frances Steloff, owner of the Gotham Book Mart in New York City, run ads for donations for him on her bulletin board. Miller had the rash assumption that he could convince *Time* magazine to run the same ad. And they did, free. He believed he could catch anybody's ear, and sometimes he was right. Such odd faith contributed as much as anything to grant him a fully bodied voice and convince me he's on the barstool next to me. Neither his misery nor his joys are exceptional, he infers; either can be had for the asking. Because it's impossible to put any kind of label on him, Henry Miller continues to be both a puzzle and an embar-

11

rassment to thousands of cultural arbiters in this country.

Perfect evidence of this is a recent biography of Miller from Simon & Schuster by a Ph.D. in comparative lit named Mary Dearborn. In a different way this biography, *The Happiest Man Alive*, is a reminder of the movie *Henry and June*, a film that could cure the horniest goat of any desire to copulate for six months. I say "different" because I can't figure out why a bloated corporation, a subsidiary of Paramount Communications, awarder of millions of dollars to several ex-presidents to not say anything about their criminal exploits, awarder of hundreds of thousands of dollars to one-fourth the Watergate crew to whine and weep and discover Jesus, memoirs that if taken collectively would redefine the word "illiteracy," should have the faintest interest in a writer who has never risen in popularity beyond that of a cult figure. If Henry Miller were alive today and walked into Simon & Schuster carrying a manuscript, he would be arrested on sight for vagrancy and trespassing. In fact, S&S regularly rejected Miller's books, as did a lot of other publishers. The difference is that, while other publishers occasionally took a chance on serious literary writing from newcomers, S&S waited until a couple of these writers emerged from the pack, established themselves as leading voices through two or three books, then, like a vulture smelling a nourishing carcass, swept in with its bags of entertainment loot and dangled six figures in front of head-of-the-pack's eyes.

When I telephoned Simon & Schuster to try to discover its rationale for printing this book, I was told by the book's editor, Bob Bender, that the publicity department handled all questions from reviewers.

"I don't want publicity. I need to talk to you."

"Who are you with?"

"I'm doing a piece on spec for *City Paper*."

"Ohhh, so you're a freelancer. . . ."

"Can you just tell me how Simon & Schuster came to acquire this book?"

"I have to go to a meeting; publicity will handle your questions," and presto the sweetest little voice south of Dixie Cup, Maine, came on the line: "Hi, I'm Millicent Milegate, assistant head of publicity on the Dearborn book. Can I help you?"

I tossed out the same question about acquisition and damned if I didn't get the same reply as Bender had given me: Who was I with? By this time I should have wised up; I should have said I was with *Time* magazine, the *Washington Post*, or the *Boogaloo Independent*.

Because when I told her I got that same suck of air with the extended aspiration on the "Ohhh." "Ohhh, so you're a freelancer." By now I understood the word "freelancer" to signal a person who runs in the same crowd as child abusers, shoplifters of March of Dimes cans, and graffiti defacers of the Statue of Liberty. Millicent, however, did have a few minutes to offer me. No, she had never heard of Henry Miller before she came across the Dearborn book, which she said she was enjoying. She was a recent graduate in English from Stony Brook.

"I'm surprised at a reputable institution like Simon & Schuster dealing with a bum like Henry Miller," I said.

"A bum? What do you mean, a bum?"

"He panhandled."

"Right on the street?"

"Yes. On the street, in the parks, door to door, everywhere. And worse . . ."

"Yes?"

"He piddled."

"You don't mean . . ."

"Yes I do. Just like a dog, anywhere he pleased."

"Ohhh my. I am going to have to have a talk with my boss. I didn't know he was that bad."

It's often assumed that the legacy of the '80s was computer chips and greed. It was not. It was the development of perfect and precious incisors in a generation of young ladies. When these ladies put the incisors into motion, it's as if each word is being minced through a screen of soft cheese. Something as deadly as "Saddam Hussein's Revolutionary Guard" comes out sounding both banal and edible. Every institution has a brigade of such ladies in its frontline trenches, their teeth polished and straightened to consumable tuning forks, their every word a reminder that there is nothing worth discovering in the whole wide world.

The other partner of this unlikely marriage born out of the wedlock of a troglodyte instigator is Academia – in the form of Ms. Dearborn. She's spent some time at Columbia and won at least one "prestigious" grant. One of her previous books, *Pocahontas's Daughters: Gender and Ethnicity in American Culture*, hints at the approach she took with 20 Miller books and 88 years of his life. At first I was not alert to this approach because I read the book from the last page forward, and in the final two pages her culminating thoughts on Miller struck me as sometimes commendable, mostly sane, and only rarely dubious. For example, she says, "His rejection of the bourgeois family and everything they stood for was heroic and hard won." That is a fair enough statement. So are these: "His compassion for misfits came from the most honest and honorable source – his recognition that their struggle against the forces that threatened to engulf them (and so often did) was his struggle as well." Or: "These years of his life stand as a scathing indictment of the way American society treats its iconoclastic artists."

Any one of these valuable statements could serve as a chapter or indeed the hinges on which to hang a whole book. But not only do words like "heroic," "compassion" and "scathing indictment" not show up again, these themes are barely dealt with, and where they are it is always in the context of Miller's brutality toward various sources. My main question was this: If a 19-year-old should ask me why he should read Miller, was there a paragraph or two I could show him that would offer some rationale as to why his work is important? Not finding any as I backtracked to page 127 – the last of the picture section, revealing a southern beauty named Brenda Venus draped around the birdlike neck of the 81-year-old Henry, who looks like he has a peach seed stuck in his mouth – I got desperate. I got so desperate, I bit into the core of the apple I was eating and came up with a mouthful of sour seeds. I spat them into the waste basket and made up my mind I would do like any "normal" reader; I would begin at the beginning. Surely, in the first 15 or 20 pages I would get some sense of why Dearborn devoted years of research and writing about an author whom most readers don't know (and those who have heard of him, think of him as the purveyor of offbeat smut).

I have to confess, then, I got a little excited when I spotted "What has Henry Miller to say to us now, in his centennial year?" on the third page of the preface. Dearborn's answer: "Isn't his work sexist and out of date? Because his books were banned for their sexual content he is thought to have been a freewheeling advocate of sexual expression. But 'freedom' is hardly the word to use in conjunction with a world view as sexist as Miller's. In fact, as feminist critics have pointed out . . ." And we're off to the races. She concludes this preface, traditionally the space allotted for discussing the worth of an author, with the following: "[H]is books can in fact reveal a great deal about sexuality and male-female relationships in our recent history. . . . Miller's writing is difficult to evaluate; he has, for instance, received no serious academic criticism. His story from its very beginning is a story of 20th century male identity." And that's it.

In other words, Dearborn has a case on her hands, a case at times both psychopathic and neurotic. And it's not merely a matter of what she sees as his sexism. He's just as often anti-Semitic, a misogynist, a sadist, a cultist (in his devotion to astrology and various strains of Eastern karma), a fascist, and in the most hilarious section of the book – which describes his relationship with June, his second wife and the June of the disastrous movie – he is nailed deftly and fervently to the cross of masochism. However, there is no evidence that Miller was ever cruel to animals, and that should give us some hope for his beleaguered soul.

There is no doubt Miller is an incendiary character to write about. "How is one to talk about Miller?" asks the critic and poet Karl Shapiro in his introduction to *Tropic Of Cancer*: "There are authors one cannot write a book or even a good essay about. Miller is one of those Patagonian authors who just won't fit into a book." It's not only the excruciating messiness of Miller's life that presents problems; most worthwhile writers' lives are full of chaos born of numerous false starts and wrong-headed decisions. Miller found more ways to fry himself than Colonel Sanders did chickens. But as he was fond of saying, a man's personality is formed from the ashes from which he resurrects himself. He spent the first 39 years of his life running around Manhattan and Brooklyn furiously trying to be a success in a dozen different careers including writing to order for magazines, and alternately thumbing his nose at them just to prove that he was, after all, exceptional. Miller had no likes and dislikes, just loves and hates, sometimes both for a person, a city, an ethnic group. Shapiro calls these "contradictions"; Dearborn refers to them as "ambivalence," but it is not the reconciliation of these "ambivalences" that interests her, not the finished work that Miller chose to offer the world, but the case against his repeated brutality she can make through unsold work, notes that went into future work, and hundreds of letters Miller wrote to friends and acquaintances.

In short, Dearborn fashions her argument much like a diligent district attorney. She rigorously follows the letter of the law through exhibit after exhibit but never captures the spirit of the man nor the writer Miller. On the one hand her mode of discourse is dispassionate; never once does she use the word "I," as if knowledge, indeed history, took place independent of the passions of men and beasts. In another sense she fairly gushes; a spate of adjectives spurts forth each time she discovers new evidence of a Millerism. If a Miller advocate can detach for a few hours, it is like watching a single member of a bucket brigade chase the incendiary Miller up and down the block. Now anti-Semitism breaks out; just about the time Dearborn gets this under control, a case of misogynism breaks out farther down the block. Then, when she has control over one end of the street, utters a sigh, and starts to give Miller his due by calling the two *Tropic* books "literature," damned if another conflagration doesn't break out from that sneaky Miller at the other end of the block and Dearborn leaves us to chase another ism. It's feverish work, and at page 266 my book burst into flames.

Shapiro cautions against quoting Miller: "The danger is that one can find massive contradictions, unless there is some awareness of the underlying world and the cosmic attitudes of the author." I say Shapiro is only partially right; the conscientious biographer could also serve justice by viewing each sentence in the context of its paragraph and then in the context of the entire book. But once a bloodhound has caught the scent of the phallic brutality of it all, there is little one can do to stop its relentless progress. Here then, is the method of Dearborn throughout her biography: on page 141 she says, "Miller had his revenge on Bertha Schrank [a married woman he flirted with] by including her as Tania, whose clitoris the narrator threatens to bite into – and spit out in two franc pieces. The book *Tropic of Cancer* was shaping up as a celebration of male identity and male sexuality."

The *Tropic of Cancer* passage she refers to is on page 5 and goes like this:

> "At night when I look at Boris' goatee lying on the pillow I get hysterical. O Tania, where now is that warm cunt of yours, those fat, heavy garters, those soft bulging thighs? There is a bone in my prick six inches long. I will ream out every wrinkle in your cunt, Tania, big with seed I will send you home to your Sylvester with an ache in your belly and your womb turned inside out. Your Sylvester! Yes, he knows how to build a fire, but I know how to inflame a cunt. I shoot hot bolts into you, Tania, I

make your ovaries incandescent. Your Sylvester is a little jealous now? He feels something, does he? He feels the remnants of my big prick. I have set the shores a little wider. I have ironed out the wrinkles. After me you can take on stallions, bulls, rams, drakes, St. Bernards. You can stuff toads, bats, lizards, bats up your rectum. You can shit arpeggios if you like, or string a zither across your navel. I am fucking you, Tania, so you'll stay fucked. And if you are afraid of being fucked publicly I will fuck you privately. I will tear off a few hairs from your cunt and paste them on Boris' chin. I will bite into your clitoris and spit out two franc pieces . . ."

The ellipses here are not mine but Miller's, and they are important. They indicate that the whole business is a mastur-bation fantasy. And fantasy is exactly what gets all the male characters into trouble in *Tropic of Cancer*. They ache to find a woman, and once they find one – prostitute, girlfriend, wife – they bemoan the fact that they are trapped. The most cunt-stricken of all this sad-comic gallery is Van Norden. "But what is it you want of a woman, then?" asks the narrator-Miller.

"'I want to be able to surrender myself to a woman,' he [Van Norden] blurts out. I want her to take me out of myself . . .'"

This is precisely the point of the whole novel. Men feel both doomed and damned by the weight of being men. They are afraid of being free; they've never broken the umbilical cord. They are in short enslaved by the idea of getting back into the womb. They do not learn, but narrator-Miller does. Toward the end of the first *Tropic* he says to himself, "Going back in a flash over the women I've known. It's like a chain which I've forged *out of my own misery* [emphasis added]. Each one bound to the other. A fear of living separate, of stay-ing born."

In fact, the "phallic significance of things" becomes a par-ody of the peter in *Tropic of Cancer*. It is neither the subjuga-tion of women nor sex itself that Miller cares about. It is the dependence on women and those accompanying fantasies that he sheds through listening to a gallery of whining men who typify the slavery to an idea (that women can be saviors) that hounds most men anywhere throughout their lives.

Dearborn never gets near the development of Miller's first book or, for that matter, any of his books. Why should she? She's got her axe to grind, and there is plenty of fodder for it; if Miller can be taken out of context, the resolutions of his contradictions ignored, she's free to write any nonsense that sucks on the sagging tit of the latest sexual politics.

Among a cascade of totally wrong statements, she writes, "Miller wanted to banish sentiment completely" (referring to *Tropic of Cancer*). According to *Webster's New Universal Unabridged Dictionary*, sentiment is "a complex combination of feelings and opinions as a basis for action or judgment." Could a man trying "to banish sentiment completely" have written toward the end of *Tropic of Cancer*:

> "Everything is packed into a second which is either consummated or not consummated. The earth is not an arid plateau of health and comfort, but a great sprawling female with velvet torso that swells and heaves as with ocean billows; she squirms beneath a diadem of sweat and anguish. Naked and sexed she rolls among the clouds in the violet light of the stars. All of her, from her generous breasts to her gleaming thighs, blazes with furious ardor. She moves among the seasons and the years with a grand whoopla that seizes the torso with paroxysmal fury, that shakes the cobwebs out of the sky; she subsides on her pivotal orbits with volcanic tremors."

This is not the obscene, trickling goo that we get in song after song, movie after movie, commercial after commercial about love. That is, love as a comfortable, harmonious prop for a dull, meager, hoarding life. Miller is not talking about Tammy meeting Blaine, complete with hand-holding and ice cream cones till death do us part. This is not the leer of the weekend sensualist who hopes a little nooky may after all lead to something important. This is not in the image of the tits-and-ass man on the page or in reality, the voyeur that Dearborn claims for Miller. This is the grand celebration of all creation in the image of a woman, not earth nor woman as the passive, domesticated fodder we've all been taught to pump for ego and profit while joining a few worthwhile causes; this is awe and wonder and rejoicing at the miracle of it all. Woman is at the center of it because she gives birth; Miller here acknowledges, as most true artists have done, the woman inside himself, a woman constantly in ferment and fermentation. In short, Miller, in this first published book of his, would have us love an earth always on the edge of fruition, always about to give birth, or, for that matter, that which is always about to explode new and whole from inside us.

If you need more evidence that Miller has feeling, read the *Tropic of Cancer* passage where he defends a prostitute against his friend's charge that she is cold and mechanical and that her pimp will only waste her money:

> "Remember that you're far back in the procession; remember that a whole army corps has laid siege to her, that she's been laid waste, plundered and pillaged. . . . It's her money and her pimp. It's blood money. It's money that'll never be taken out of circulation because there's nothing in the Banque de France to redeem it with."

There is surely more sympathy here and understanding on one page than Miller gets from his definitive biographer in an entire book. Not only does *Tropic of Cancer* have "sentiment" on every page, but it's the sort of sentiment you get from a man who's bled himself of every last vestige of the conventional feelings that alternately keep us trapped within ourselves, saddled on the conveyor belt, and deranged at the thought that our lives are sailing by without much of anything happening inside us.

Mary Dearborn, for the academic life of her, or perhaps

because of it, has no idea what Miller is up to. For her he is a sort of period piece, dragging his overstimulated gonads around the earth, the dusty wake of which attracts a few thousand clods from the "liberated" '60s, climbing aboard his literary phallus and crying "Ship Ahoy" on an ocean of sperm, till Kate Millet comes along in 1969 to set the record straight and restore a modicum of justice to this pariah of women and his coterie of Hugh Hefner clones. "Few would deny the greatness of his Paris books," Dearborn says. But what, exactly, is the nature of this "greatness"? We never find out, but we get hints. Here is one: "The theme of his greatest books is survival, for Miller was first of all a survivor."

That word "survivor," like many of the words she gives the greatest weight to, are buzz words of the '80s, part of the dreary and forbidding lexicon of a stampeded decade. Christ, Mary, Dickie Nixon is a survivor, and he's the best used car salesman we never had. I can walk up any alley in America, the hallway of any institution, and find shells of human beings who have more or less survived. I can start at Columbia University, continue to Congress, and follow a long and sleazy trail to Santa Fe, New Mexico. That's where John Ehrlichman lives. John's doing quite well, thank you. Thanks to advances for books published by our ole buddy, Simon & Schuster. Miller's books aren't about being a survivor at all, Mary. In fact, in one of those books of his that you call a "small success," *The Air Conditioned Nightmare*, Miller addresses that word:

> "Few are those who can escape the treadmill. Merely to survive, in spite of the set-up, confers no distinction. Animals and insects survive when higher types are threatened with extinction. To live beyond the pale, to work for the pleasure of working, to grow old gracefully while retaining one's faculties, one's enthusiasm, one's self-respect, one has to establish other values than those endorsed by the mob."

No, no, what we have in Dearborn are precisely those values endorsed by the mob, granted a mob well versed in all the tactics of analysis, articulation, diplomacy, and marketing. The mob I'm talking about splinters into competing groups each week, though all its members have been shaped by the same forces; all clamor for media attention, all speak in shrill, strident voices. Last week it was the Mothers for Abused Little Leaguers, this week it is the Society for Dispossessed White Fire Fighters setting up picket lines in South Albany, Georgia. Tomorrow the Cousins of Cancer Victims will parade in front of Congress. The Jewish Defense League has little interest in baseball or mothers or, for that matter, Lenny Bruce. The so-called feminists (are any of them truly feminine?) don't mention Thoreau or Dick Gregory or Chekhov, who in a letter to a friend said, "There are times when I awake full of euphoria; then I go down to the street and hear a woman's story and grief overwhelms me." Black leaders see no point in the visions of Black Elk, and the smoldering Indians on the Rosebud reservation haven't the faintest idea who Toussaint L'Ouverture is. The environmentalists read tracts, not poetry. But the most indicative remarks about what's really going on in this society come from the mouths of babes. More than one of my students when I taught at Howard University advised me that Richard Wright made a mistake in making the hero of *Native Son*, Bigger Thomas, a dropout. "He should have been a lawyer, then we would have listened," one girl told me, and a number of other students in the class nodded.

There we have it. It is not vision that counts, but correctness – the code of a society so physically and spiritually mangled you won't meet two people in a given year who know how to walk. The center of gravity in the stride of a U.S.er is in the shoulders. His real hero is the middle linebacker from Notre Dame. For power is what it is all about, not the real power born of experience as it filters to the bone marrow and out again in hard-won articulation, but the specious power of GROUP. Not the GROUP of community, which has

22

a common and noble purpose but the GROUP that wants to aggrandize itself because every member has had his ego pummeled since the day he entered first grade. Not the GROUP that approaches the microphone with a certain caution and with hesitancy as to how it will phrase its grievances, but the GROUP with the pent-up rage of a mob, demanding this and demanding that but asking little of itself as GROUP or as individuals. "More jobs! Education!" is often the battle cry, but Miller, as well as the other visionaries listed here, knew the jobs to be at best a form of masturbation if not downright destructive; education taught us how to vote for one among a series of idiots indistinguishable from one another. In a group of 20 freshmen at Howard, I was lucky to meet one who was ever encouraged to write or talk about his experiences by one of his previous 50 teachers. What replaces the language of experience and reflection upon that experience is the language of Slogan. The same as TV, newspapers, our daily conversations. Shortcut language in the feverish race to arrive at a goal titled Society's Stamp of Approval. In the meantime, our ears and noses blow out the car window. Never mind, we're in a state of frenzy at a loss we can't remember, but just ahead . . . just ahead is the exit number for the town of our final arrival. We can't remember the exact number because it gets all confused with the lottery number we played this morning. Life is always happening just outside of us. To start the day, we read the *New York Times* or the *Washington Post* so we are versed in the group-think of separate grievances. We don't begin by wiggling our toes in the grass or staring up and marveling at the sky or carrying *Native Son* to work with us. That would be bad for business. Bigger Thomas, as both a creation of Richard Wright's bloodstream and a piece of independent magic, sees and talks with more power than a thousand Ph.D.s in comparative literature. The entire population of lawyers in Washington, D.C., could fit into his back pocket. Yet if Bigger Thomas wanted to get away with murder today – granted, an accidental one – he wouldn't have to retreat to the rooftops of Chicago. All he would have to do is attach a Walkman to his ears and look numb, walk a puppy on a leash, or pretend he was jogging. The cops wouldn't stop him, nor would any biographer label him a misogynist. You see, Bigger would be offering those evidences that he was thoroughly domesticated, every ounce of the wildness necessary for a vision of happiness and peace gutted out of him by the time he was 12 years old. His struggle to be a man is what we most fear. What Dearborn most fears about Miller. Because she and we are reminded that we make a game of life rather than playing it for real, thus making ourselves shells long before our deaths.

To the young today, Orson Welles is that hustler for a fruity vine, Dick Gregory has a fat farm in the Bahamas, James Earl Jones is the voice on CNN, and Paul Robeson sang gospel songs. Lenny Bruce ran a dirty mouth during a freer time, Emma Goldman inspired commies and did time, Helen Keller invented Braille, Eugene Debs inspired workers during a time when they had no rights, and Henry Thoreau liked to walk in the woods and commune with nature. The casual vacuuming of a casual history of *isms* and sects as it arrives in our living rooms beside the *crepe de carnage*, the Beaujolais, and the stereo offering us a string quartet from heaven. With each passing generation more domesticity sifts down, the passing faces on an average day more seared with rancor and underlying bafflement. We say, "You can't yell fire in a crowded theater," as I will be accused of here. We don't remember that Justice Oliver Wendell Holmes said it upon sentencing Eugene Debs to a year and a day in prison for telling young men not to sign up for the draft in WWI. We don't remember Debs' response either: "Your Honor, I was advising young men not to enter a building on fire."

Henry Miller advised us that the whole world was on fire, as well as his heart, the latter unnecessarily so. Like Debs, he asked us not to get burned. And for this he was and is sentenced with silence and anonymity. When someone like Dearborn steps forth on the privileged support of several powerful institutions to speak of Miller, she rolls us a severely and diligently polished imitation pearl from the persistent vacuum of her own guts and the institutions whose creed she has adopted. From the shallowest depths, this pearl whispers, "It was just a momentary jarring. The man was a mess. Go back to your indentured comfort and everything will be all right."

To whom does the future belong, the three or four Millers who periodically come along, or the legions of Dearborns with their brilliant expertise and inherent cruelty? The answer is neither.

In no field today would we even recognize a leader who could show us the way out of the morass we have gotten ourselves into. Real power abhors a real vacuum, and don't think for a second that the foxy résumés of the Dearborns fill this vacuum. The real power will come in the form of the Crips and Bloods and a dozen other gangs fighting over turf. The difference is that the turf will be the suburbs, the universities, Wall Street, and the airports. Everywhere. These gangs' notion of power is as imitative and reactionary as Dearborn's, the Pentagon's, that of the whole link of institution to institution and the institutional thinking that dominates the U.S. But there's one important difference. They are willing to put their bodies on the line. They have not been funneled through institution after institution so that they can sever word from deed. These are the left-out ones who snicker at the mention of school. What can any teacher teach them, who have organized and plotted and robbed and murdered and lived as if each day were their last. They know in the bat of an eyelash that no adult has anything to offer them, that words from adults are just so much ca-ca running down the side of a building, a building like Simon & Schuster's on the Avenue of the Americas, where they could never enter except through the use of force. And they know the world is run by pure force, not words, not vision, not the poetry of Miller and Thoreau. They don't want any part of the system except to pillage in it in order to create their own system. And their own system will make the SS look like disciples of Billy Graham.

I got a primer on this one the other night on the PBS show *Hate*, chaired by Bill Moyers. During an hour and a half of one expert after another, from John Kenneth Galbraith to Elie Wiesel to the psychiatrist Robert Jay Lifton, experts reflecting on dozens of groups struggling for equality, only three people emerged with any insight into the origin of hatred. The rest circled and circled hate in a dazzling gamut of abstraction.

One of the three was a former Israeli soldier who beat and dragged a Palestinian boy onto a truck in front of his parents. He was later so horrified by the expressions on the faces of those parents that he changed his identity. He reinvented himself in the form of a Palestinian and experienced all the injustice, physical and psychological, that he'd formerly inflicted. "The worst part," he said, "was not the physical abuse but the sense of being a nobody. Even when people were nice to me I had the feeling I didn't exist." What I want to emphasize is that this man experienced the denial of himself not as an Israeli – he'd switched identities – nor as a Palestinian – he could always revert back to at least a semblance of his former existence – but as a man marooned, an individual. Now, on PBS, he speaks as a man living between cultures, a no man's land, as it were, as a true individual. His body was denied in previous times; if he is to rediscover his body, and the beginnings of freedom, he must approach the world as an individual reaching out for other individuals.

Is this not what Miller was saying? Gregory, Thoreau, Bruce, Goldman, Whitman?

As Miller points out, if anyone comes along to sing "The Body Electric," he is quickly fitted with a skullcap and marched to the electric chair at Sing-Sing prison.

Unless, that is, he sings on behalf of GROUP, a group determined to be as ruthless in its defense and propagation as the next GROUP. Thus enter our final two witnesses, the head of the Crips and the head of the Bloods. Both spoke of hatred as beginning and ending with the body. "Once you deface your enemy in your mind, it's easy to kill him because he didn't really exist before the killing," said the head of the Crips. He added, "It's just like you sending boys to Vietnam and telling them to kill gooks. They're gooks, they don't have faces. Well, it's the same for us with our enemies."

There is no doubt that the Crips and the Bloods and a hundred other gangs mean to turn this hatred inside them on the world; they are already doing it. There are no men and women around worth the name to stop them, and had there been, there would not have been cause for the Crips and the Bloods to have been born in the first place. For two centuries now we've been resisting every fresh voice that came down the road, labeling them this and labeling them that, even as a former civilization created layer after layer of slave society and for all its sophistication received as its reward Huns and Visigoths. Do we deserve better?

kiss me, I'm still alive: on irving stettner

If you want to wake up happy in the morning, read Irving Stettner. If your nerve endings are frayed, your mouth dry, and you're alone because your mate just flew the coop with your best friend's mother, read Stettner. Stettner will flush your liver, tap on your nasal passages, and make your hormones burgeon like overripe plums. You will wake in the morning feeling a lightness, openness, and generosity you haven't known in years. But such attributes here in dear old Weenyville can only make you subject to arrest. No longer rigid with YIP's syndrome (Yuppies In search of Power), you can only take up residence in a jail cell, but make certain to take a copy of Stettner with you.

For Stettner is the original street urchin. And has remained one for 70 years. He is a man without a Social Security card because he has little interest in security and he has never bought the noxious socializing process that informs most of our souls. He lives out of two suitcases in one-room apartments where the gas jets on the two-burner stove are clogged from the overflow of pea soup.

He has no car, no insurance policies, no Walkman, and only the faintest notion of how he will earn his rent due the following week. A helluva way to live, you say? No, the joke is on us, for Stettner's life testifies to the power and joy we could achieve if we lost our fear of poverty. In the words of William James, "Our stocks might fall, our hopes of promotion vanish, our salaries stop, our club doors close in our faces; yet, while we lived, we would imperturbably bear witness to the spirit, and our example would help to set free our generation."

That is precisely what Stettner's work bears testament to – "witness to the spirit" – or, more precisely, a spirit that keeps his head raised and his eyes and ears delighting in much of what he sees and hears. The term "memoirs" isn't quite appropriate to his non-poetry works. They are little philosophies of action that form a consistent whole. Their genesis is not literary inspired, but comes from a desire to be alive. We are born to take part in life, not to drain meaning from it, not to arrange it in preconceived forms. Moment-by-moment impulse and a constant alertness to everything that has fullness and movement are the heart of Stettner's writing. He has retained the joy and wonder of childhood in a country that specializes in turning out perpetual adolescents who have lost every virtue of childhood. In short, Stettner is an innocent traveling among a nation of parasites. He creates; we consume, convinced by all sorts of idiots posing as experts that the "creative spirit" belongs to a select few who are first sent to "gifted classes," later take advanced placement English, and eventually win a National Book Award, a Booker Prize, or a Nobel. This is the approved version of "creativity" and acquaints us with all the mannerisms of art but none of its power. "In real art," says Picasso, "painting, isn't an aesthetic operation; it's a form of magic designed as a mediator between this strange, hostile world and us, a way of seizing power by giving form to our terrors as well as our desires."

Today, readers and writers are trained alike; language is a form of deflection, not a way of "seizing power." To be a real reader or a real writer, one would have to both burn off the institutionalized forms of dead grass, as the Indians used to do, and recreate new ways of approaching the written word.

Because our lives have become so abstract, so removed from both earth and heaven, we offer each other opinions and arguments, not stories.

As a parallel to the breakdown in literature, and by way of showing the strange route Stettner has taken toward discovering both life and the written word, let's take copulating. People complain to me all the time about the treatment they get at the hands of the opposite sex. Women complain about

the deviousness of men. Men complain about the deviousness of women. Both sexes complain about their inability to
find good fucking. In a world where the inflation of language
makes all subjects spurious, it's the one topic people agree is
worth talking about.

Yet, never do I hear from people that the approaches to
fucking are all screwed up. By approaches, I mean the places
and avenues through which we meet our potential copulating partners, namely the workplace, bars, and parties. Each
of those little meeting places fosters a language which is
doomed to efficiency, and the cunt and the cock and true
art abhor a language which is efficient. The language of efficiency ignores the passions and thwarts the pituitary. It is a
language that fosters not creativity but equivocating: "Maybe
yes, and maybe no, and everywhere all over. Where did you
say you worked?" Equivocating is the language of business.
The language of business has only one desire: to find a sucker.
As President Coolidge once said, "The chief business of the
American people is business," and it was a statement more
prophetic than any a poet uttered in the 20th century.

The bars, the parties, and the workplace don't establish
warmth or intimacy. They are as cold as any meat locker. No
wonder then, in a place like Weenyville (Washington, D.C.),
it is possible to meet thousands of handsome people, well-
educated, finely tuned to the arts, the men speaking in the
crisp modulations of a Gregory Peck, the women as poised
as the queens of the soap operas, and not discover a drop of
juice in any one of them. To hear them talk after seven beers,
you'd get the impression they could take on a chorus line or
the Green Bay Packers in a single night, but all the physical
evidence suggests they would be better off at home with their
computers.

Now you see why all that is called serious literature is up
Shit Creek. The approaches to writing, as with the approaches
to copulating, are totally wrong. Born in the schools, students
of writing travel a vertical route through layer after layer of

equivocating, which is to say the business of art is business; you can be as funny and truthful as you want, but if you don't make a good buck, or at least win a few awards with your stories, you can go fuck yourself. We'll all stay at home and hump our Apples till we learn the art of proper equivocating. A Washington, D.C., restaurateur named Benny once advised me, "Where you have money, there's no action." The man spoke wisdom.

Year after year, Jonathan Yardley of the *Washington Post* bemoans the breakdown in contemporary American fiction, but you won't catch Jonathan reviewing Stettner's work. Yardley's assertions to the contrary, he rarely reviews small press work. He doesn't search out good books to review; he reviews what comes to him. And what comes to him are the same frozen meat lockers for literature that are offered to us to find our potential fucking partners: hardback books from the big conglomerates in New York and Boston, accompanied by publicists' handouts.

This, in turn, is backed by nationwide distribution, the co-operation of the bookstore chains, the economic clout of the wholesalers, the tepid and sniveling readings and workshops at the universities, and finally the you-pat-my-bum-and-I'll-pat-yours kind of reviewing that goes on in the major newspapers and magazines. Periodically a Yardley is held up as a legitimate critic and offered in defense of the criticism that a place like the *Post* is going soft. Yet, Yardley is no different than the Gregory Peck modulators at parties who, after seven beers, quack "There is no good fucking in this town." Presented with a good book or a good woman, they couldn't recognize it as such, and if they did, they couldn't get a hard on anyway. The gulf between word and action has been legitimized. Indeed, the whole system by which we drowse in our comforts and pick our noses depends on it.

For the exact meeting point where the institution of reviewing and all the other institutions meet, I'll let Kurt Vonnegut talk for a while. In an April 29, 1990, letter to me, Vonnegut discusses a particular review he wrote for the *New York Times* and, by implication, how that institution functions: "I wrote a review of Tom Wicker's book about Attica [the prison riot in which scores of inmates were slaughtered], and they knocked off the last third of it without first telling me. The last third was about why Wicker cried when the shooting started." The *New York Times* doesn't want tears from a grown man. It's afraid of tears, terrified out of its living skull of tears. Nor does it want real joy, real despair, real anything. Where all the institutions meet is their utter fear and dismay at emotion. Animal or human, sooner or later they find a way to shoot emotion.

Thus, there is a superb irony here. Though the artist begins from emotional impulses, the institutions designed to support art have a chronic and perverse fear of emotion. If more than a hint of the raw emotional life that goes into a painting or a novel (or the messiness at somehow surviving while you get your creative work accomplished) is displayed, the supposed benefactors of art and artists run from the room, mumbling, "Taste, what's become of taste?" The adventurous artist will not find support among art institutions, and rarely among his supposed fellow artists. No, he will find it where he least expects it: the food and beverage manager at a dreary and pompous hotel chain, a computer expert, a hairdresser, the checkout girl at the supermarket, the bakery women – black and poor and overworked – at the same supermarket. Such people have not bought the official line on art. Though they have limited means of supporting art, they know it must originate in the heart. They often write poems or paint pictures which remain hidden from even their families and mates. This is not a world which looks on the amateur with much respect or sympathy.

To be called a real artist, a "professional," you have to get your work out in front of people and get paid for it. To earn this prestigious title, both the artist and his work must first be screened through an elaborate daisy chain of de-genitalized idiots with the right connections, all of whom believe art is a civilizing maneuver. It has become respectable to be an artist, and the artist in turn must be respectable. The number of people who want to be writers or painters is legion, each of them so brain-dead, they are ready at a whisper to pare their overwrought emotions to manageable proportions if only it will ensure, if not success, a little respectability. Respectability is when you get in on a group show or when you place a poem in the magazine *Swollen Tendril*. Never mind what the gallery or magazine, newspaper, arts council, or university ultimately stands for. "Get me some attention and legitimize me, or I'll piss all over my neighbor's petunias," the fledgling artist says to himself.

The extent to which the artist must be respectable offers no better example than our long-neglected subject under the microscope here, Irving (Oivin to his friends) Stettner. Early in September, I got a call from a faculty member at UCLA named Snyder. This is the centennial of Henry Miller's birth, and in the last week of this month writers and professors and others will be celebrating him with seminars and conferences up and down the West Coast. Snyder said he was part of a panel that was going to discuss the legacy of Miller. He had read my essay on Miller, and wanted to know if I would be willing to serve on the panel. This discussion stalled when it became uncertain whether UCLA would be willing to put up travel expenses. At some point in the conversation, I asked Snyder why he didn't invite Irving Stettner to this conference on the legacy of Henry Miller. His response: "Stettner's a bit scruffy, isn't he?"

Never mind that Stettner had exchanged more than a hundred letters with Miller; never mind that Stettner was one of the few people that Miller thought of as a real friend; never mind that Stettner's tiny literary magazine *Stroker* was one of the few in which Miller would publish his work in the last three years of his life. And never mind that Stettner has written and painted brilliantly all his life, that he has had to find his audience by going from café to café, bar to bar in New York's Lower East Side, including Alphabet City – one of the most drug-ridden and dangerous places in America – hawking his paintings and books. A dollar here, a dollar there, anything to stave off the landlord for another week. Stettner, with his bulbous work shoes and broken umbrella, plods along in the rain, looking for someone to put a touch on, while Snyder, in casually mussed tweeds, smokes his pipe, chirps to a classroom full of students about the "mavericks of art," and casually blows smoke out his ass.

Ten days after our phone conversation, a packet arrived from Williams. In it was a videocassette entitled *The Henry Miller Odyssey*, a film portrait of a "diabolically truthful man" by . . . Bill Snyder. Much of the film centers on Miller's Paris days, when he begged, borrowed, and stole to survive and produce those books that some people call "art," days when it could be surely said of Miller that he was "scruffy." Miller from his grave and Stettner from his easel are chuckling at such whorehouse shenanigans as celebrations and seminars. They know that as soon as a writer gets invited to such things, he is dead. Surely the brochure produced for the celebration illustrates Céline's statement, "Every virtue has its own indecent literature."

Even more deadly is the language of equivocating that reduces everyone to the same level. Fear reduces language to a steady, dreary sludge of ambiguity; is what the American Melting Pot is all about. Everything and everyone is flattened under the ethic of efficient modernity, which finally adds up to downright worship of The Machine. Listen to the low rumble of slick, cunning, evasive language coming from the mouths of everyone concerned in those televised Senate hearings on the confirmation of Clarence Thomas. (In 1991 Thomas was a conservative black who was eventually confirmed to the Supreme Court despite controversy over supposed sexual harassment of an employee ten years earlier.) Listen to these hearings and you realize this is the language of fife and fickle, foam and dome, and till death do us part you'll never know what I'm thinking. It's not merely the flattening of human fiber and bone, but the steady, cautious erasure of every vestige of human personality. It is the language of the professional workplace, not in the service of expansiveness of blood vessel, but padded non-talk to win a grant, protect a position, create an image. In such a hopelessly gray world as the workplace, there is nothing else to do but periodically cry, "Long Dong Silver." In such a world, everyone is harassed because every human being is interchangeable with every other human. No one counts, only the system, a system that has no use for the direct language, the rage and delight of Whitman or Thoreau or Stettner, only for the bubble-gum language of law books written by men with hippo jowls, laws entitling them to stuff more poison down their gullets.

The whole point in getting powerful jobs is power, to be boss, to make others obey their will, leverage in the service of ego, and, yes, sex. "Up on Capitol Hill, they used to fuck right on the desk tops," offers a lawyer after several drinks one night, who said he had 15 years' experience on the Hill. "Now, with all the flak from discrimination and sexual harassment suits, they take them to a hotel room."

In 1991, most Americans are afraid of strangers; the one place where they overcome their fear of other people is the workplace. Work is where most people make their social base. This explains why marriage, initially born of at least some small intimacy, quickly degenerates into a business partnership. The language of equivocation wins out entirely; each partner pretends the other doesn't have genitals, let alone a sense of humor. Then, divorce, and the whole process begins again. But, this time around, the beleaguered divorcee swears he is not going to invest so much of his heart. He'll invest his energies in a career where the heart is not as much at risk. Career is the language of law books, business manuals, and academic jargon. If the pulsations of groin beckon, our career soul has only to interrupt them before they get to the heart, before they involve the whole person; he has only to bark at some underling, "Wanna see a picture of a chicken going down on a stripper?" Of course, dear underling could always say, "It's chickens who should be eaten, and preferably fried. Now cut the shit and hand me that file folder." But underling doesn't. She answers in the professional jargon of ambiguity; her whole training has been not to offend the boss; besides, only through such language can she advance her "professional" career. She says, "At this point in time, I believe categorically that the civil rights of both the chicken and the stripper are in jeopardy." Boss is sitting there thinking, "Is this bitch for real?" though this is exactly how he would phrase the issue if he were not in rutting season. "Maybe she is putting me on, maybe she's in heat too and this is just code talk for 'I'm available'; I'll ask her out and maybe then I'll have some idea where she's coming from." And on and on.

Nobody in that Senate committee room (Clarence Thomas confirmation hearings) had the faintest idea what anybody was saying. Constantly they asked each other to repeat a question or an answer; explanation was offered to explain explanation, and with each succeeding drone and dribble of cautious rhetoric, they dug a deeper and deeper hole. Of course the senators can't make a decision; neither can we. The wrong people are on trial. The people who should be made to defend themselves are Thomas's and Hill's law and writing professors at Yale. They would each be given three minutes to tell a story – not an argument – that everyone could understand. If they failed to do so, Ted Kennedy could step down from the rostrum and yank out their tongues with a pair of pliers.

Watch the faces of the senators, particularly Kennedy. They are bored to tears. For 40 years they have been listening to such horse shit. They are bored with their jobs, bored with so many words, bored with all the toxins their livers are spewing up from too much rich food and booze. When Anita Hill said, "I was both disgusted and embarrassed," it didn't register. Only when she got to the part about pictures of animals and Thomas' alleged references to his prodigious dong ("Long Dong Silver") did they perk up. All the rest was a charade for our benefit, to get our vote, and more importantly to convince us that it was business as usual. The real obscenity was that most people have been conned out of their very lives; these same people sat and watched these assholes for hours at a time, fully trusting that the legislation they draft next week or next year is going to protect them in some way. Along with Kennedy, the senators and a good portion of the viewing audience were all so sunk in tedium that inwardly they were smiling and wondering to themselves, "Just how big is this guy's dick?" Where quality of life evaporates, quantity rears its sniveling head. It's called objectivity. "We are gathering all the evidence we can so we can arrive at an objective decision," one senator cried from the podium. Yes, you can be objective, senator; you can go home and pound your pudding in a bucket of Mother's Oats.

But if you, the reader, want to know what is really going on in this capital of capitals, listen to this 25-year-old graduate of the University of Chicago, recently arrived in Washington, D.C., to work in one of the many "think tanks" that abound here: "Washington has a way of attracting the most intelligent young people and then co-opting their intelligence into the existing system. Each day I go to work, I realize it's all a lot of bullshit. My job revolves around my boss. The other day, he handed me a pass to a meeting at the White House; the week before it was two tickets to the Kennedy Center. I get paid well, and there are always these perks. The whole point is to follow on the boss's coattails because he has the connections to keep your career moving. I know it is all wrong, but I don't have an alternative vision."

It may be that this young man does not have an alternative vision because he hasn't gotten miserable enough to desire to look for one. He is a devoted reader of offbeat fiction but apparently none of the books suggest to him that he might live differently. Probably these books are called "Literature":

they are clever and they amuse him but they are, after all, just books. What he needs is a tonic that would give him another vision of life and develop in him the patience to develop a language to support that vision. He needs writers and painters like Stettner.

But as I've shown here, Stettner does not count. He is "scruffy." He is outside the system. If you want to advance in a career, image is what counts. Along the way, you had better find the specious, insulated, non-language to support that career.

If our young friend wants an alternative vision to dependency on the Boss and the Boss's accompanying conveyor belt of smugness, comfort, and utterly joyless existence, he might glance at the work of Stettner. Stettner is the antithesis of everything the young man has been taught. He is the opposite of the wall to knowing yourself or to the world as I have described it.

Stettner is more a descendant of Mozart and Chagall than any writer. He is 80 feet off the ground, and at night he floats over the rooftops of Paris, Manhattan, Tokyo, and LA. The sky is blue-black; there is a full moon; and there is Stettner, playing violin on the rooftop of his favorite whorehouse. In Colon, Panama, he falls in love with a prostitute, and stays in love with her even after she gives him two doses of the clap. Is Stettner a fool? Of course! But no more a fool than a Chaplin, Keaton, or W.C. Fields. He is the eternal innocent who takes life where he can find it and always makes a song of it. "He looks on the gorgeous side of shit without ever denying that all of us have a very difficult life to live these days" says Seymour Krim (also a remarkable writer) about Stettner.

It is not that he has blundered into that soap bubble that says, "Let's look on the positive side of life," but that he is insistent on being faithful to an endless curiosity and exuberance and, above all, to maintaining a freedom of movement unshackled by the bread cupboard or by ideological enterprises. He is that rarest of creatures, a free man. By free, I mean he has faith – not faith in the religious cliché of that word, but faith that he can find both in men and in nature the expansiveness that will make him feel glad to be alive. And Stettner finds it everywhere.

But mainly he finds it in the street. If Stettner has a religion, it is The Street, accompanied by the son and the holy ghost of The Incident and The Stranger.

Anywhere in the world now, the entire machinery of education, government, and media is devoted to one thing: convincing people that the streets are dangerous and that they should stay home and, by inference, turn over their lives to some polite, sophisticated, crackpot institution (i.e. themselves). Occasionally, in some rap song, I get a notion that there is something to be learned in the streets besides bloodshed, but no other medium advances such subversive knowledge. Take away the streets and you take away freedom of movement, people's innocence, their right to gaze, create, respond, discover anything new. If the 19th century is the study of how the people, often in a misguided form, took the streets from the king and queen, the 20th century is the study of how they returned the streets to a series of "democratic" institutions that supposedly represented the interests of the people, but found increasingly ingenious ways to get people off the street. They have succeeded, because most towns and cities in the U.S. at 6:30 on any given evening are deserts of concrete and glass. Cross the border from Mexico into the United States, and cleanliness and order strike the eye, not life. The great science of the 20th century, then, is not nuclear fission or aerodynamics but crowd control refined to the point of crowd elimination.

Control the streets and you control how people eat, shit, fuck, and count their money; you control how people think and feel. In a stadium or concert hall, there are walls; the crowd is contained; the same with a university, office complex, or shopping mall. Only the street offers a free flow where there is easy means of entrance and escape. Like the arteries of the body, the street can literally sing with fresh infusions of blood, or it can get wounded, become infected, and bit by bit have its various limbs develop gangrene. It doesn't just die, the dead part is chopped off and thrown on the scrap heap. Thus, in addition to crowd control, which is the duty of every true professional, the next most proliferating science of the 20th century is surgery. This surgeon comes in the form of doctors, cops, hangmen, prison wardens, and teachers. All their training teaches them to be objective. Only the funeral parlor director is objective. Surgery and crowd control become one and the same thing.

Most of the supposed revolutionaries, including Marx, who want to dynamite the blockaded ends of the streets to allow a true flow of blood, have been another in the series of surgeons and crowd control ignoramuses. They don't want a free flow of blood; they want type A blood or type B blood, never circulation. The rubble from the explosion of this or that political fixation creates new blockages under this or that fashionable label, and the whole dreary process starts again.

"Europe, it seems to us, is also close to saturation and aspires, tired as she is, to settle, to crystallise out, finding her stable social position in a *petty, mean mode of life*." [italics in the original]. This statement was made in 1852 by a wandering Russian named Alexander Herzen. Does it not describe the United States today? The "settled" or "stable social position" can be observed in any bar where the patrons stare up at the television like catatonic zombies to gauge the progress of the latest competitive feast; or in any classroom where students sit with their notebooks folded, their hands folded, their brains folded, waiting to "be turned on" by some card-carrying Ph.D who folded up 20 years ago; or in any office where the recipients of patronage wait for the boss to give the word on which color toilet paper they should wipe with this week.

It is all the same. We are all the same. Waiting like Godot for some one or some thing to turn us on. Make us feel alive, like we're breathing, and blood does really flow in our veins.

We sit, waiting for the cry of "Long Dong Silver" to break us up, make us laugh and applaud with relief, because in that small portion of our hearts still receiving blood we know the public obscenity and the private will are one and the same, reducible to a stale joke. Any other cry, any other language with a hint of intelligence and imagination couldn't penetrate our brains, loggered as they are with bad air, bad beer, bad pizza, insufferable slogans, and not the faintest notion of what it is to be a human being.

"The life of a student is more full of incidents and proceeds much more stormily than the sober, workmanlike life of the father of a family," Herzen continues. "A life without incidents, sometimes diverted by external impulses, would be reduced to a uniform rotation, to faintly varying *semper idem.* Parliament would assemble, the budget would be presented, form improved . . . and the next year it would be the same, and the same ten years later."

Stettner does not have the problems of sameness because he is a seeker and a giver who employs his trade on the street. He is a sidewalk sketch artist, and as such, his life is filled not with just strangers, but with an alertness to the amazing variety of human beings. Without such an awareness, an affection for the bonding of the eccentric and the bond broker (as Balzac often saw), we go mad. We become numb and intolerant if we cannot find and love the peculiarities of eccentrics as they nibble the sharp edges of Dollar and the assumptions of people who have Dollar.

Often, before he made his rounds of the Paris cafés to sketch people, Stettner warmed up with trees, flowers, and plants in a nearby park. Then, when he sketched people, he saw them in another way: "If I ran into the most nondescript, ugliest mug imaginable: I was always able to find one feature, at least – I simply looked for it – which had a spark of beauty to it." This is not arresting beauty for the sake of money or simply a Pollyanna outlook to spare himself reality; Stettner understands that the source of energy, hence his own salvation, is located precisely at some detail of grace. Let the grace of a chin or pair of eyes blossom and the whole person has a reborn look. Thus, Stettner's flatteries become suggestions for revival. The only problem was that people took on a slightly hollyhock look after he had been to the park. When he looked at people he saw flowers, and his clients stared at the finished portraits "perplexedly a few minutes, until they finally shrug their shoulders, and smile indifferently, as if chalking it off to my uniquely individual style."

What excitement Stettner feels when he has a good day – is able to feed himself, have a glass of wine, knows he can stay in his hotel room another two days. And what an embarrassment to us who make nothing, who shuffle papers with a dead language to validate other papers equally dead, and return to our apartments assured of eating. Stettner grows while we languish, feasting on public issues we think will lend our lives importance.

The best part of The Street is that incident leads to incident, stranger to stranger. He meets a bookseller, who in turn leads him to a Greek artist named Kosta. Kosta rips the young Stettner's assumptions about life while paying him money to sketch the streets of Paris: "Artist – gad, you don't even know the meaning of the word . . . Also, you're an American; that's nine strikes against you. You think . . . you can do everything by pressing a button . . . no patience! . . . And *you* meanwhile. It's getting so cold, you said, a little while ago, 'tomorrow you're going to wear two sweaters.' Imagine! My, my . . . . Why, do you know the kind of men in whose footsteps you're following? Giotto, Van Gogh, Gauguin . . . Guys who tore their guts out, and slapped them on to canvas!"

At age 18 or 25, we should all be so lucky to have such a virulent and invigorating criticism to wean us from our whining. Hah! Try such uncompromising language on a group of young people today and they will telephone their lawyer fathers to press for a "harassment" lawsuit.

What evolves in Stettner is a devotion to moment-by-moment living – the air, the sky, food, the flow of a particular woman, wine and the variety and quality such things yield. He is not looking over his shoulder to see if a grant, a gallery showing, an editor waving a contract are pursuing him. He goes to Tokyo and the small towns of Japan:

> "The Japanese women. Yes, just to be able to sit opposite one in a trolley car was an experience in itself, unforgettable. There was the full round rich moon oval of their faces, each with its delicate finely chiseled nose and mouth, and the slanted jewel eyes."

He goes to Colon, Panama: "I remember Avenida Bolivar, its long, wide-open main street with its unique heavy sweet smell of chicory, dust, dung, mangos, and palm fronds all in-termixed, the swinging louvered doors of the porticoed bam-boo shops and bars, the hot sun beating down like a laughing gold tom-tom, the high shoeshine parlor chairs right out in the street, the shoeshine boys' lively chatter in broken English and Spanish."

Stettner is sort of like horseshit: he turns up everywhere, except that unlike manure, his eyes and ears and heart get bigger and bigger, the writing a little more patient with each volume, without sacrificing the exuberance or sharp details that capture the essence of place-family while growing up in Brooklyn; the utter vacuum of the streets of Los Angeles as he knocks on doors, a kind of Fuller Brush salesman. He wears the pavements on his sleeve, and he is pure tonic because he is conscious of the vitality, even when it's deranged, within the bullies as well as the more kindly souls of this earth.

These portraits of people and places are written the way Stettner makes pictures: quick, bold lines built around two or three central features and colored with his enthusiasm for the subject. Like Henry Miller, Stettner gives me the feeling of a companion chatting away. But while Miller is content to rap away in some café corner, Stettner is perpetually looking for space. The movement is from the streets and doings of men and women to the tops of buildings, trees, sky with its own incessant change. In particular he loves the sea; it is natural that he spent several years as a seaman. The world of the sea and sky is much more tolerant of rhapsodizing – of growing wings and taking deep breaths – than office buildings or subways.

The stories in these books are not just about survival – the hand-to-mouth existence of hundreds of odd jobs and survival's relief through a painterly vision of the heavens – but about the men and women in his life who have helped shape a voluptuous attitude toward daily activity. A couple of the men are famous, like Miller and Stieglitz, but mostly they are unknown – construction helpers, seamen, unknown artists, whorehouse madams and their charges, a zany uncle, two teachers, and a music shop owner. They are distinguished and held together by a Mediterranean attitude toward life. By their robust affection for food, wine, the human body, and protest in action against injustice – not just in words – they keep Stettner earthbound and from settling on a cloud with his Aeolian harp. On the subjects of manhood and art, they freely dispense advice to the young Stettner. Just as valuable, they are always buying the little fucker something to eat. Between Miller and Stettner, I swear the prerequisite for adventure and art is an empty stomach and an equally empty wallet. Everywhere Stettner goes, he gets himself adopted.

Alfred Stieglitz is famous now as a photographer and as the husband of Georgia O'Keeffe, but 50 years ago his gallery on Manhattan, An American Place, was lucky to get two visitors a day. One of those was young Irving. When Stettner complains to Stieglitz that he has no money to buy a Mann painting, the owner says to him, "Never mind, someday you'll pay the price."

"What do you mean?"

"Everyone pays – sooner or later. One can't receive without giving in return – in one form or another. Especially you – since you're born with a gift, and quite a precious one, too, like a jewel, which sooner or later you'll have to give. Or share, rather, since that's what gifts are for. It's simply your fate: you'll be miserable till you do."

Stettner doesn't understand what Stieglitz is talking about. His memoirs, then, can be viewed as the attempt to fulfill his advisor's prophecy, to understand the nature of what he has to offer and the price he must pay for answering his destiny. Nowhere is he more miserable than when he can't summon the courage to marry a beautiful Japanese girl named Emiko, with whom he has fallen in love. He loses not just the girl through his own cowardice but a whole way of life he loves just as passionately as the girl.

As Emiko presents herself the first time, she is pure grace and sureness, an antidote to Stettner's descriptions of American life, which is often pure bullying and arrogance born out of confusion:

> "She dropped to her knees, and, head erect, with slow and graceful gestures served us tea. Bright auras of jeweled silence seemed to float around her. . . . I was entranced, speechless: she was like a flower, a tiger lily or chrysanthemum, swaying at the end of its long stem . . . one of those women who don't have to speak since their faces say everything: enigmatic, exquisitely beautiful, totally feminine, yet feline, demonically so. . . ."

She releases in Stettner his first desire to draw in three years; he draws his love and presents it to Emiko's family.

> "I watched them as they eyed it with broad, appreciative smiles. What a difference, I reflected, between their reaction to my pencil sketch, and that of my own parents back in Brooklyn. . . . My mother and father would have regarded it with total indifference. Either that, or they would deeply wrinkle their foreheads and roll their eyeballs heavenward, as if uttering a silent prayer, as if I had only presented them with a grim omen of my fate: in life I was headed straight for the penniless gutter."

All this takes place a few months after the U.S. dropped atomic bombs on Hiroshima and Nagasaki. Emiko's parents would have had every right to close the door to an American soldier trying to woo their daughter. Instead, they treat Stettner with courtesy and hospitality, and it's not because he brings chocolate and cigarettes (mediums of exchange in postwar Japan) to their home. It's because he is sincere, handles himself with tact, and offers curiosity and respect toward their way of life. On his last evening with them, he thinks, "ahead lies a shaky wooded house which shelters a few friends with whom I've known the first real happiness and contentment of my life."

Yet, Stettner is easily convinced to turn his back on his love and her family. It was necessary in those days to get the permission of the U. S. Army if a soldier wanted to marry.

"Who's the gal?" a captain queries him.

"Emiko Yamada."

"You don't mean a Japanese girl, do you?"

A friend of Stettner's, a private like him, is just as bad.

"Just think," he says, "How are your folks going to feel – if you bring home a Japanese girl?"

Of course, now, 45 years later, the Japanese have had the last word. If they reneged on buying up our Treasury bills, issued quarterly, the entire U.S. economy might fall on its face in a matter of weeks.

Not only has young Stettner still not understood Stieglitz, but these magical sketches of post-war Japan serve as a cautionary tale. They undercut any facile romanticizing of Stettner's life. Few people realize at the time who or what is of real value. It is only when we build space and reflection into our lives that we understand who can best serve us and what we have to give to gain new value. This takes money and a simpler mode of life, because it takes at least some money to buy the *time* to evaluate what is best for our lives. Someone like Stettner, living on the fly, not sure where his next shelter is coming from, dashing from city to city, country to country, uncertain of his values, loses track of who and what is worth keeping. I believe in many instances it is only in the writing that he rediscovers those gems that have slipped from his fingers. It is a hugely sad story, this tale of the lost Emiko and the patience and tolerance she might have brought to a frantic man's frantic life. But it is no less the story of the United States, a country looked to now for 150 years as the salvation of starved and drained people all over the world, but a country, for all the chit-chat about its melting pot ambience, which has little interest in alternative ways of living.

This is the nagging thread Stettner picks up on in his memoirs. From 1946 to 1968, he runs around the U.S. and half the world snatching for this alternative vision that Emiko first alerted him to in heart and flesh and not just the dictums of Stieglitz. He goes from one job to another, trying to filch a little time to paint and write. His reflections go back to his childhood and the handful of characters and oases within the factory desert of Brooklyn. Most prominent among these are his mother's remarks about a local bum-drunk, whom the child Stettner judges to be disgusting in his louse-ridden clothes and incessant babbling. When he complains to his mother, she says, "You should feel lucky being able to sit with him. He used to be a musician, and a great one, too." It's little incidents like this that set off reverberations throughout Stettner's memoirs. Increasingly he drifts toward the company of oddballs – the drunks, the mad, the eccentric, the floaters. In 1968, Stettner claims his passport was conned from him by a U.S. Embassy official promising a free trip from Paris to New York. The U.S. government refused to return it for 15 years, thus grounding Stettner on the Lower East Side. There he survived through a hundred odd jobs, wrote and painted out of a one-room apartment, and hustled his wares among the bars and cafés of that area. It was there that he began a lively and profuse correspondence with Henry Miller and started a literary magazine called *Stroker*. "Miller must have found here [Lower East Side] a strong degree of comfort," he says, noting the "verve, humanness, and European mellowness" on Second Avenue.

Nearing 70 and still in good health, Stettner has recently moved to Shaverstown, Pennsylvania. He says he is working on more Paris memoirs. But I feel it is the years 1968 to 1991 he should deal with. I say this because there is a difference between the innocence of one's youth and "earned innocence," a term invented by Nelson Algren. It is comparatively easy to be light and carefree at 24 or 34. During these years, Stettner is a promising artist. But the United States specializes in and cultivates youthful potential that never comes to fruition. Look at all the one-book authors – Styron, Mailer, Heller, Salinger (one and a half), etc., etc. But how does anyone keep their gusto, verve, humanness when the gray hairs settle in and he has an artistic audience of 14, eats out of tin cans, and buys coarse toilet paper instead of White Cloud? This is what I mean by earned innocence.

In short, how is it that the boy becomes a man, shakes off the mentors and becomes a true voice in his own right? To some extent, in his poems Stettner indicates he has retained wide open eyes and a clear, singing voice, but I still feel the fuller treatment that only prose offers is needed to fill out his self-made suit.

I could go on and on about the magic of Stettner, his joy, and his refusal to whine though his material circumstances have been difficult. But the fact is Irving Stettner could not sell his paintings and books on the streets of Washington, D.C., or any other city in America.

He would have to have a vendor's license. Cost – $1,106. That's right, $1,106: $1,000 as a refundable cash bond held by the city should he poison us with a vision of a different kind of life and $106 for a license to sell on our cherished streets. True, he might camp under the protection of some friendly bar or restaurant owner or bookstore manager, but it is the more sympathetic and adventurous business that collapses first. We don't want life; we want power, and we want it fast.

The streets have been turned over to two extremes: the real estate speculators and the banks, who have the full support of the corrupt politicians who control the zoning boards; and the teenage street gangs and the drug desperadoes, who are going to cut our throats if we don't hand over our purses or wallets, fast. Though Stettner lived on the Lower East Side of Manhattan for 30 years and was considered a legend there, he can no longer live there. It is too dangerous. "Hell, let him sell his books at Lincoln Center," you say.

Four years ago I witnessed what happens when a writer tries to sell his books at Lincoln Center. Now, New York's vending laws exempt writers and painters, but the police don't know it. On the day I stood beside a newly arrived writer from Toronto selling his self-published novel, four cops hopped out of a cruiser and asked him if he were selling religious books. "Only religious books can be sold on the streets," they told him.

"My book has a spiritual quality," he told them.

"Don't start that intellectual shit with us; get out of here."

He started to gather up his books and display stand, but not fast enough for these contemporary enforcers of what is correct marketing on the streets. One cop pushed him and, when the writer protested verbally, gave him another shove and tripped him. Then the other cops joined the first cop in giving this "unprofessional" writer a few kicks to the ribs. When I jumped between them, I was handcuffed, thrown in the police car, and eventually booked, along with the writer, for disorderly conduct.

The charges were finally dropped, but before we left the station, the cops said, "Keep your asses off the street and this kind of thing won't happen."

Why didn't he or I protest this to the proper authorities?

Why didn't Anita Hill (assuming for a second she is telling the truth) protest "sexual harassment" at the hands of her boss?

"I don't understand," says one senator, "why in this city of all cities, Washington, D.C., where there are so many avenues for redressing grievances, why Anita Hill couldn't have come forward 10 years ago with her story." Because, senator, from the age of two, we are all taught we are little people. Until we are two, senator, we are taught to walk and talk. After the age of two, and for the rest of our lives, we are taught to shut up and sit down. The airing of our "embarrassment and anger" over an injustice at the hands of a superior conflicts with this dictum. From the age of two all we are taught is competition. Winners count, not losers. Power, not language, not true vitality, is what counts. It is not the police or the drug gangs who are to blame. They are the reactionary tools of "professionals" like Snyder, who finds Stettner too "scruffy" to include in the party. They are the tools of the well-housed everywhere who use language like "at this point in time," a phrase first popularized by John Dean 16 years ago during other nationally televised hearings. Murder space and time through the "fashionable" use of language and you close off the streets. Now we are just a phrase away from viewing all people as alike under the banner of correct political and racial and sexual thinking. We are ready to assign our emotions to the banner of our "professional careers" and their accompanying language of equivocation and "objectivity."

Now, now, Henry Miller's statement that "Only murderers have profited in the 20th century" makes absolute sense. Close off the streets to people like Stettner, and the cops and the kids are licensed to maim and murder.

Mayor Sharon Pratt Dixon could win "the drug war" in one week. All she would have to do is turn loose 70,000 10-year-olds on the streets of D.C. Let them sing their songs, paint the sides of buildings, dance in front of the restaurants, shout their poems, and run up and down Dupont Circle, playing the flute and the oboe. And let the police escort them in the rougher sections of town. Put the circulating blood of creativity back into the streets and watch the natural "high" that everyone gets. But such an idea will be written off as pie-in-the-sky romanticism, a crackpot notion from a crackpot artist.

Besides, anything involving "art" is consigned to the "appropriate department," but it's the departmentalization of everything that leads to the strangulation of the creative will. Sharon Pratt Dixon, no more than any other supposed leader, has no more idea of what keeps the blood flowing in a city than she does in her own body. She, like the rest of us, has been trained to hate the body. It is a tool, something loathsome that must be hammered into submission to sit at a desk, a committee room, a job, to mouth inanities; but the body has no value in itself.

We are immune to the world of Stettner. We hope he will go away as we hoped Miller, Bukowski, and a thousand other artists would go away. Many do; they go to Bomb School, inject heroin, drink themselves to death, join a guerrilla group in Peru. More often they go to Yale Law School, which goes on their résumés just underneath the MBA from Harvard at about the same time as their dicks and uteruses flop in the wind like freshly washed socks hung out to dry. "Long Dong Silver!" This cry goes up in school and marketplace, private office and public hallway, and its obscenity is matched only by another cry that brought us from the streets as children to congregate around the latest gadget in the snug bosom of our homes. This was the radio, and the cry was "Hi Ho, Silver!" Silver was the Lone Ranger's horse, and the Lone Ranger was a masked man who, aided by a dirty Indian who did all the dirty work, went around the frontier administering justice. No one ever saw his face, and he never hung around after his noble deeds to even accept a "Thank you, masked man." Except for Tonto, he was always alone and he dispensed silver bullets as his calling card. Henry Kissinger told reporter Oriana Fallaci in 1976 that he felt "like the Lone Ranger" when he was sneaking out of Washington at night to go to Paris to negotiate "peace" with the North Vietnamese. But who was Henry's Tonto? Us? Because if the Lone Ranger took Tonto behind a boulder at night and took off his mask, and there was genuine love between them, then everything's fine and I'm full of shit. But if the Lone Ranger just fucked that Indian in the ass so he could shit silver bullets in the morning, then we're all fucked. There's nothing left to do but show each other pictures of chickens going down on strippers.

And if I seem demented in reducing the world to one great asshole, all you have to do is turn on the ABC's *World News Tonight*. According to Peter Jennings and two other reporters, sidewalk artists such as Stettner are not dead. No, not by any means. They vigorously survive on the coasts of Southern California and South Florida, where they charge $16 to $22 for a quick sketch of you . . . or you and your Tonto. There's one small catch. They won't draw your face . . . or even the front of you that might hint at the heart . . . or the genitals. No, you have to turn around, for these masters of the latest ideological vernacular are "Butt Artists." The ABC reporter made a big deal over "butt," persistently trying to egg the artists toward a more decorous name such as "rump" or "buns," but as one of the artists explained, "It is what it is and we call it 'butt.'" Goodnight, wherever you are, holding your ass in your arms, asshole.

his own best friend: on charles bukowski

Charles Bukowski mumbles better than other writers declare. Like W.C. Fields, his least movement, smallest utterance jars the prevailing quiet and order. He is an order unto himself and wherever he steps, whatever he reaches for, a dish falls, an old lady carrying a Bible is bumped, a merry-go-round of insanity is released. Though both men possess extraordinary physical coordination, they are also chronically absent-minded. Out of a paranoia about the motives of others, they hide money under the rug, under the ice-cube tray, in books, and then can't remember the next morning where they put it. Chaos ensues. They throw up their arms, they curse God and Walt Disney; they tear apart the house. Once, upon returning books to the library, Bukowski spotted something green peeking out of one book, and opened it to find three 20s and a 10-spot, a huge amount of money for him at any period in his life.

This absent-mindedness isn't for lack of concentration; Fields' and Bukowski's concentrations are simply elsewhere. They find the world odd, and beneath all the hijinks of their respective art forms, mostly loveless. There is little that endures and little that isn't pervasive quackery, and both men have a barely concealed loathing for the experts. What endures in their work is not so much any exalted notion of the primacy of the individual, but the pure difficulty of becoming and remaining W.C. Fields or Charles Bukowski.

Both men struggle prodigiously for some sort of equilibrium by trying quietly to locate an inner harmony, a small corner of the Earth where they can be left alone. They step out of the lonely claustrophobia of hotels and rooming houses to find a touch of human company in bars. Both have rotten nervous systems and alcohol is their sedative, and finally their poison. "Happiness," Fields once observed, "is quiet nerves." Both men pay a phenomenal price for burning off layers of false ego to get down to the essential nugget of personality unfettered by convention. Both artists have been battered as kids by Prussian-type fathers swearing allegiance to order, cleanliness, and a new refrigerator. Neither has ever had a sense of home except the inner cavities they created themselves: fantasies full of calamity brightened by their abiding sense of the ludicrous. This takes detachment and, for large chunks of time, a heroic separation from personal interest to gauge the nature of humans.

The problem is that the other bar patrons quickly pick up on this separateness. There is nothing like self-containment to arouse the suspicion of other human beings. As Bukowski once observed:

Not Wanting Solitude
Not Understanding Solitude
They Will Attempt to Destroy
Anything
That Differs
From Their Own

Black glances are fired their way. Silence invades the Perverse Pussy-cat Saloon. Knees jiggle against the bar fronting. "A stranger is among us," is the unanimous consensus. What to do with him?

"Where did you say you were from?" a regular might ask Fields.

"I didn't but as long as you mention it, I'm from Punxsutawney, PA," he says, dwelling lovingly on all of the syllables of groundhog town, where he has never been.

"What brings you to town?"

"Nutmeg convention," Fields says proudly.

Soberly, the interrogator nods. Hostility is dissolved; men raise their glasses but there will remain a lingering bafflement at his presence, periodic glances his way.

The utter sobriety of patrons, even in a bar, is the point. It reduces them to a density and gullibility that's incredulous. It makes Fields and Bukowski chirp like a pair of canaries on a barbed-wire fence. People are constricted bags of barely animated features that release in the two artists a gaiety that dominates all of their work.

Like Fields, Bukowski is mostly a counterpuncher, though he has little of the comedian's hyperbole. The world isn't just ludicrous for Bukowski; it's half-maimed, and the flopping part of people that remains more or less alive is positively cannibalistic. Everywhere people are devouring each other and spitting out the indigestible remains.

In his movies, Fields shaves his truculent vision down to the absurd rituals of domestic and middle-class life with only a hint of the personal pique of poisonous residue of a society built on deceit. The world is all pomp and fraud and Fields punctures its balloon in one burlesque after another. An innocence akin to Dickens remains, and though men often admire someone like Fields, who has a low opinion of humanity, the comic vision must be palatable: The bite should stay at the level of ha-ha. It shouldn't make people slow down and ponder their lives. That's per 20-minute short or 60-minute featurette. Yet, when you take the total accumulation of Fields' work, you realize he was playing it for a great deal more than the laughs. He distances himself from anything that might be called realistic and comes up with a truer picture of the U.S. than a hundred *Taxi Drivers* put together.

In thousands of short takes, poems, stories, Bukowski does the same.

At a glance, this work often appears as "slice of life" portraits of tawdriness and betrayal with a bizarre and deftly ironic twist. However, taken cumulatively, his 40 books produce a total picture. It is dark – people find ingenious ways of lopping off bits and pieces from each other and themselves – but it's finally as redeeming, invigorating, and, in these bludgeoned times, as necessary as fresh air.

If I have insisted on coupling two very disparate results, it's because Fields and Bukowski are two of a dozen of the truly unique U.S. voices of this century. Their lives and their work are instructional manuals on how to convert paranoia into galvanizing art. Manuals that can't be imitated. Fields and Bukowski eschew any sort of orthodoxy, not because they are rebels, but because they are so busy being themselves. Beyond their 50 feet of space, the world doesn't exist for them. They patrol that 50 feet with the vigilance of big cats, always with booze in hand. Fields hides in the bushes in the Hollywood hills, a bottle of gin in one hand, a highly erratic gun in the other, waiting for a mythical burglar who never appears. Twenty years later, a few miles below in an East Hollywood bungalow, Bukowski peeks out the blinds at any knock or strange noise in the street. He doesn't answer the door.

Both men make venturing out to the sidewalk a heroic act. The streets are a disaster, and never for a second does either man doubt that there isn't someone waiting out there to do him in. Fields' specialty is dogs. They instinctively sense his separateness from the species that feeds them, and bound after him as if he were a rabbit. Most notable among Bukowski's pursuers are women of the type who shriek "Scratch his eyes out!" on Channel 50 wrestling. They have three-inch-long fake fingernails and have applied their lipstick so ferociously that they appear to have been screaming all their lives.

A second type that Bukowski attracts might be called the "Literary Groupie." This creature, historically, has been well fed but resents it. They see in Bukowski's material deprivation the necessary ingredients for cooking up "poetic soul." They telephone him at 3 a.m., announcing in a theatrically hushed voice their admiration for his work and their willingness to drive to his place at that moment. "I read one poem and I knew you had soul. My husband's out of town. I think you'll like my poems." As much as a fourth of his output is devoted to getting rid of such women – after the itch of loneliness and gland has been sated. Sometimes they get rid of each other as happens in the poem "Who the Hell is Tom Jones?" An older woman enters his place to attack a younger rival while Bukowski's narrator surrogate sits, bemused and drunk, in his shorts. At one point he tries to separate them but he is 55 years old and no physical match for them; he wrenches his knee and retires to the bathroom to admire himself in the mirror and take a long-overdue shit. The two women shriek and claw and batter each other up the block. Squad cars arrive, as does a police helicopter. It was "better than the Watts riots," Bukowski announces. The poem ends with two cops leading the torn and blood-and-piss-bespattered older woman into the bathroom where the cautiously joyful author sits on his throne. They "wanted to know why. /pulling up my shorts! I tried to explain."

Though Bukowski will occasionally rant in full lyric rage, he is mostly the calm eye at the center of a hurricane. Especially in his later work, he parries the world with a deferential jab, feigning only modest interest in the latest enterprise foisted upon him. His opening lines often begin with a fake yawn. "Here we go again." This makes his pursuers lead with their heads which Bukowski continues to poke with a vaguely interested left. The men in his living room exhaust themselves, usually in confessions of failure, in an hour to an hour-and-a-half. In one poem he times their monologues.

But for the women he waits even longer. In life and in writing, his supreme virtue is patience, his favorite rejoinder, "Have another drink." Liquor reduces his ladies, and most everyone else, to a comatose state while culling in himself a calm resolve and a razor watchfulness. In a poem called "sticks and stones" Bukowski summarizes this resolve:

> complaint is often the result of
> an insufficient ability
> to live within
> the obvious restrictions of this

god damned cage.
complaint is a common deficiency
more prevalent than
hemorrhoids
and as these lady writers hurl their
spiked shoes
at me
wailing that
their poems will never be
promulgated
all that I can say to them
is
show me more leg
show me more ass –
that's all you (or I) have
while it lasts

and for this common and obvious
truth
they screech at me:
MOTHERFUCKER SEXIST
PIG!

as if that would stop the way the
fruit trees
drop their fruit
or the ocean brings in the coni
and the dead spores of the Grecian
Empire

but I feel no grief for being called
something
which
I am not;
in fact, it's enthralling, somehow,
like a good
back rub
on a frozen night
behind the ski lift at
Aspen

The childhood chant of the title goes "sticks and stones will break my bones but names will never hurt me." It's part of his personal history that he's been called every derogatory name known, beginning with the repeated accusation of "FAILURE" from his father, and later echoed in a thousand rejections from women and editors because his face is ugly and his writing reflects an ugly world. Now in his 60th year (at the time of the poem), he has built his world and his armor against such accusations. The Bukowski world has always had an insistence on physical detail, especially if it can he related to the body. Our credos, ideologies, homespun decencies, in fact, most words fly out the window when presented with the body. He knows words become rationalizations for denying the body and eventually slaughtering it. The body doesn't want to be marched off to numbing jobs, calcifying marriages, frontline trenches; the body wants to march to bed. Mostly in bed (though occasionally at the track, or the classical music on the radio, or in a bottle) do the few bits of honesty, love, and beauty we still have within us rise to the surface.

It is in bed (with a bottle never far away) that the Myth of Bukowski is born, the myth minus its essential ingredients. From Tokyo to Munich to the queenly hallways of Vassar and back to Los Angeles, feature writers with douche bags for brains pump the myth of Macho Man. He is shown on the cover of this magazine and that feature section. To some extent, in letters and in public performance, he pumps this hype even as he rails against it in poems and stories. And even as magazine texts make the obligatory connection with Hemingway, "The Old Man and His Cock," there has never been a more unlikely subject for media hype than Bukowski.

Bukowski was writing for 30 years before the media came sniffing into the carefully arranged clutter of his living room. One time, early in the hype game, in trying to uphold the Macho Man Myth, his 55-year-old body rebels. Trying to screw a woman standing up, he throws his back out of place. Even before the first twinges ("the end of a short affair"), he is thinking "138 pounds, 138 pounds." After the woman leaves, the pain is so severe he drops a glass of water. He then places himself in a tub of hot water and Epsom salts. The phone rings. With excruciating pain, he manages to extricate himself from the tub and reach the clamoring phone. It's the 138-pound woman.

> "I LOVE YOU," she said
> "thanks," I said.
> "is that all you've got to say"
> "yes."
> "eat shit!" she said and
> hung up.
>
> love dries up, I thought
> as I walked back to the
> bathroom, even faster
> than sperm.

Thus, the court jester, the fool for all seasons pulls the string on this farce to guillotine the most dominant word of the 20th century. Love excuses the need to be sensitive or responsible, thoughtful or kind; each day almost as many murders are committed in the name of love as for country. Supply each person using the word "love" with a machine gun and soon the word love would equal the plagues of earlier centuries. It's not a matter of disparaging "love" per se; Bukowski longs for it periodically, searches for it like the rest of us, and occasionally finds it. It never lasts long and he doesn't blame anyone. The live ones – male or female – are clawing for some support system; the half-alive are propped on mannikin stands by little industries that are spurious and tyrannical in themselves. The world is a madhouse, and none of the schoolbooks or songs, *isms* or sects even attempt to prepare us to accept ourselves let alone the banal and carnivorous doings outside us.

What Bukowski has then, is what he has had all along, and

what he always returns to – acceptance of his solitude. It is painful, and particularly in his early work he writes like a man hanging from a 20th-story ledge. But at least it allows him to have moments when he can see and hear in the mad juxtapositions of daily life what is really going on. Just as important, this solitude of his keeps him from becoming one of the "neutered faces glistening;" he gets to be that rarest of creatures – a personality not extinguished. He gets to be Bukowski.

I have written as if the seeing and hearing of daily life and the integrity of the personality reflecting in solitude are different things. They are not. At least not for Bukowski. Where other writers end, he begins. Most writers (or filmmakers for that matter) circle their material, hoping to extract a nugget of illumination, intimacy, true feeling from their subject. Bukowski's solitariness and gargantuan inner detachment won't allow him such conventionality. He's already up inside his material, looking out and at the same time outside, watching Bukowski trying to maneuver for his daily sustenance. It's the sort of daring that lands people in nut-houses, jails, or city morgues. The shock to our systems then, upon initially reading Bukowski, is the encounter with someone talking to us from the other side of the mirror. "Love dries up, faster than sperm." We smile with the shock of recognition. But what an awful thing to say, we think, what an overblown generalization. But even as we think such thoughts, we know we are reacting from habit, from the way we have been taught to think, the way that will continue our paychecks, the soft soap job for our next piece of ass, the language of lies we hope will steer us toward somebody affectionate and lasting.

Bukowski will give us none of our habitual reflections. It is not through pronouncements he speaks to us. Not the screech of the rebel flailing out at the system, nor the beatnik heeding the call of the open road.

He has the luxury of speaking to us in a quiet, conversational voice because he is the insider, and we, with our accustomed comforts and our shopping carts full of lies and our

61

pursed mouths ready to rage at some unlikely undeserving victim, are on the outside. Bukowski has walked away from the reflections that supposedly instill a sense of well-being to convert space into time and time into freedom. The work moves so leisurely; it ambles. Like Einstein, he seems unmoved by time. He takes the measure of everything so casually, yet so surely. He is in and out of the material in a few pages. It all seems so easy; how does he do it?

He does it so easily because he's back behind the mirror, inside the belly of terror. He tosses up bits and pieces of its body, and we smile or laugh out loud with recognition and say, "This guy's a bit much." It's not a matter of Bukowski describing terror and the night; he is the night, sinuous and not very approachable, his lightfooted ambling a reminder of a self we forfeited long ago.

If I have rambled here at some length, it's because the vultures are circling the still-alive meat of Bukowski as they are doing with the bones of Henry Miller. The catalyst for combing the toejam of these men is of course a film, what else. Because schoolbooks are no longer the innocuous burblings they once were, and now are well-wrought clubs of oppression and repression, the citizenry is turned off books altogether by the age of 12. Also, the maniacal pace of life and people's capitulation to it have a lot to do with the ravings over the most sugar-pap films. A strong book requires the active participation of the reader. No less than the author, the reader must lay aside his social ego for a few hours to enter a new world. Not so with most films; a tether is floated to the exasperated mob, giving them an image to chortle over and try on the next day at the office, or that evening with the recalcitrant Wendy.

The movie that resulted in the Bukowski "renaissance" was 1987's *Barfly*, directed by Barbet Schroeder from a script by Bukowski and based on an early part of the author's life. I haven't seen it, but I do know it started the boys at editorial desks in several industries salivating. All hailed Bukowski for being "on the cutting edge of the dark side of the avant-garde," but what they were really hailing was their prescience on when to cash in the chips on yet another asshole who had the gall to think he could make a living writing from his gut.

As was the case with Miller, a New York commercial press that won't get near Bukowski's writing has seen fit to publish a biography about him.

"My first day on the job in a mass-market paperback house I had the distasteful job of being told to reject Charles Bukowski's *Notes of a Dirty Old Man* with a form letter," wrote the pseudonymous C.B. Coble in the January 1984 issue of the *American Book Review*. Coble, a commercial house editor who worked in a dozen publishing firms, concluded his rare blast from inside by saying, "What passes for publishing in essence has become lowest common denominator merchandising, with a few carefully 'controlled' deviations thrown in as a defense mechanism against meaningful criticism. Some will argue that publishing is a business. Granted. Everything is a business by 1983. And that includes the survival of basic values we once took to be self-evident." But this is a little different than our daily lives where we rarely telephone another person unless we can use them. As Bukowski notes:

> attrition rules
> most give
> way
> leaving
> empty spaces
> where people should
> be.
> and now
> as we ready to self-destruct
> there is very little to
> kill

It is not a matter of me fussing about systems – publishing or others; merely to walk down the street is a criminal act. We

all should have been screaming from our rooftops the healing power of Bukowski, Miller, Giono, Himes, Fields, Keaton,
Holiday, Bessie Smith, whoever, a long time ago. But . . . but
the neighbors would have frowned. They would have heard
us, gone inside, farted – and mistaken it for a mouse – and
called the cops. Lip service to decency strangles us.

The author of *Hank: The Life of Charles Bukowski*, Neeli
Cherkovski, is an awfully nice fellow, and in this book about
his ol' buddy and one-time partner in a small-press venture,
he pretty much loves everybody. Hank's (Bukowski's nickname) a success; his madness, his war with all that is mean
and petty, his facial ravages from acne vulgaris have all been
vindicated, and now here is Random House getting on the
bandwagon, offering the final *Good Housekeeping* Seal of Approval for that mad dog Bukowski, at age 70 finally tethered
to his kennel. So get out the beer and lintburger sandwiches,
we're going to have a party, gang.

At first glance, Cherkovski avoids the travesty of a number
of recent literary biographies, most notably those on Henry
Miller. He doesn't seem to be bound and gagged to the pil-
lar of respectable constipation that dominated the Mary V.
Dearborn and Robert Ferguson books on Miller. Cherkovski
is a poet and has been part of the West Coast literary scene
for a long time. He is hugely sympathetic to Bukowski's work
and the war the writer has gone through to produce his little
time bombs. There are several good sections to this book, and
yet on successive readings I always come away with the same
feeling: Neeli Cherkovski is incapable of putting the Bukowski achievement into words.

On the surface, both the lively and dull parts of this biography present an interesting phenomenon: Where Cherkovski
has men around on which to build his narrative – Bukowski
himself; several small-press editors who launched Bukowski;
John Martin, the author's longtime publisher at Black Sparrow Press; and *Barfly* director Barbet Schroeder – the writing has authority. It is crisp, and the content is relevant at a

perfunctory level. But when he has to shift to the women in Bukowski's life, the energy flags; his heart skips first one beat, then two, then three; he loses interest; the prose deteriorates into one cliché or near cliché after another until it reads like a script for *As the World Turns*. "The loss of Jane [Bukowski's first love] darkened Hank's skies," he tells us.

Far more serious are those interludes where Cherkovski must take the stage – without the presence of Bukowski's backers – and address the nature of the author's work. To his credit, Cherkovski refuses to fall into the trap that Random House was expecting – the raunchy exploits of a beast that would rival the sleaze of the *National Enquirer*, all under the brand name of literary avant-garde. Periodically he keeps calling attention back to Bukowski's work and quoting chunks of it. Fine. But what does he make of it all? Is there any particular reason why we need Bukowski? Why read him?

If, as Schroeder correctly notes, Bukowski can't be identified with any outsider movements in literature, how is it that he surfaced at all through the clotted jungle vines of the herd mentality, nit-picking, risk-disdaining, degenitalized literary scene of the United States? True, Cherkovski chronicles his publication history, but this doesn't explain why Bukowski's readings would draw 400 to 500 people in the '60s and '70s, when name poets would be lucky to attract half of that. Most of Bukowski's audience were involved in one or another of the protest groups of that era, yet he thought both public protest and groups a waste of time. "They got into the anti-war movement because they're lonely hearts," he told Cherkovski then. "They have no ideas of their own. These same people, if they were in control, would be just as bad as Johnson or Westmoreland." Then, what binds Bukowski's audience and his large readership to his writing, if at the social level he's so out of tune with them? And what was there about the '60s and '70s that nourished him into prominence?

It would be impossible for a Bukowski to emerge in 1991 and garner the following he mustered in the '60s and '70s.

Yes, small presses with ambition, taste, and originality in their design spring up each month, but like their cousins at Random House, these publishers and their editors have all sworn allegiance to Junior Scholastic in the seventh grade. The role then of John Martin at Black Sparrow Press is all the more important. Without John Martin there is no Bukowski. Where several previous small press publishers had located a readership of 400, Martin over a period of time got him 400,000 readers. About Martin, Cherkovski says, "Martin had already secured (by 1969) himself a permanent place in the history of American letters." Fine. But how? What obstacles to Bukowski did Martin overcome to get him nationwide distribution, publicity, or performing at such august colleges as the University of Michigan?

Among other questions not addressed are these:

Why does Bukowski receive the adulation of a rock star in several European countries, yet is still relatively anonymous in this country? Is it the media image of "the dirty old man," or do those German and Italian fans see his work as establishing an intimate relationship with their own aspirations? As Bukowski's German translator and promoter puts it: "Writers in his own country had a built-in censor, as though the spirits of the great classical writers were looking over their shoulders." But the U.S. isn't exactly loaded with uninhibited writers; writers here may not have "great classical writers" hovering over their shoulders but that hasn't kept their censors from being as "built-in" as anywhere else.

When Cherkovski does attempt to place the work and Bukowski in some sort of perspective, it reads like the prose-style of a jacket blurb writer at a New York publishing house: "Poems poured out of the great myth maker." "Bukowski's prose had the same kind of lean imagery as Henry Miller's. The sense of Whitmanic man prevailed, unattached to ideology. . ." "He became a patron saint for these wild, young minds. . . " "He created a literary hand grenade to lob at the academy . . ." "He had not relented in his poetry, road maps for the man's daily sensibilities." "Jon and Gypsy Lou [early publishers] were *survivors* [emphasis added], like Hank himself." "I watched him move along with that Bogart stroll of his." "I guess the key to the secretive Bukowski lay in his gentleness, which he masked beneath a tough-guy exterior." And don't forget the Lone Ranger and his little girl, Tonto.

Cherkovski insists on coupling Bukowski with Whitman and Miller; at the same time, toward the end of the book he readily agrees with Schroeder that his work "had little to do with the Beat aesthetic, Henry Miller, or other 'outsider' movements in literature." If Cherkovski really believes this, why didn't he go back through his manuscript and qualify more carefully Bukowski's loose affinity with other break-through spirits, and then tackle the essence of the man? He does make brief headway in his interpretations of individual prose and poetry bits, but then quickly gets lost in more liter-ary jargon talk, stuff like the "universality of man."

If this were simply a case of a well-meant but flawed biog-raphy, I would say, fuck it, and go lay in the sun. But there's something insidious here and it's this: Thoughtless adulation can cut the balls off a true voice just as handily as critical judgments spun to the latest sexual and political hysteria.

No sooner have I thought that thought than an idea even more grim shadows it. Neither Random House nor any other commercial publisher (and let me add 98 percent of the small and university presses) could have dealt with a manuscript that took the true measure of Bukowski. Cherkovski's insulat-ed literary non-talk is acceptable to them, though the carnival barkers at Random House would have preferred something a little more scandalous.

I was reminded too of a conversation I had with one of Bukowski's German publishers some years ago at the annual German Book Fair on the island of Manhattan. When I asked this publisher why Bukowski's books weren't on display, he said, "My New York contacts in the industry think he's too crude. Of course, in California it's a different story."

His explanation is partially true; yet the affluent, whom those "New York contacts" sense, have their crudities and perversions like the rest of us. The difference is that the people who are willing to pay $27 for a book want their perversity clearly labeled "Serious Literature" on the bookshelves where the Trumps and Kissingers and the Goodeyganders can see it; and "pornography" at the back of the hall closet behind the china for special occasions.

Then, someone like Bukowski comes along and the "crude" is all mixed up with insights, for example this insight into what makes a woman a truly memorable human being: "There was something warm about her. She wasn't constantly thinking about being a woman." Or this insight into what makes a man dull: "Looking at my father I saw nothing but indecent dullness. Worse, he was even more afraid to fail than most others." An insight into language when writers like Hemingway use it: "Words weren't dull, words were things that could make your mind hum. If you read them and let yourself feel the magic, you could live without pain, with hope, no matter what happened to you." Hundreds of small insights attached to the rage of an acne-pitted 18-year-old trying to find some small corner of the world not dominated by "dull, trivial, and cowardly existence." This novel, *Ham on Rye*, written when Bukowski was 60, culminates its many wisdoms in a passage in the middle: "The problem was you had to keep choosing between one evil and another, and no matter what you chose, they sliced a little bit more of you, until there was nothing left. At the age of 25 most people were finished. A whole goddamned nation of assholes driving automobiles, eating, having babies, doing everything in the worst possible way, like voting for the presidential candidate who reminded them most of themselves."

No, the objection to Bukowski has little to do with the "crude." If such passages as I've just cited were taken seriously for a minute by the hardback-buying elite, the $25-a-plate sturgeon at Barney's wouldn't seem so appetizing, the

$200-an-hour prostitute or wind-up dildo would lose its urgency. For a brief moment, the labels, by which the affluent and their minions the cultural arbiters wrack and stack the world so that their beef may be a bit more tender, their nooky more comely, their face lifts and breast implants and group sex protected under the watchful eyes of security guards at São Paulo, Bahamian, and Cancun hotels, are thrown into confusion, and they must wonder what it is to be a human being, what their brief lives on this earth have amounted to, if anything. If their children came across Bukowski's work, they would surely have a moment when they wondered whether to run away or blow Mom and Pop away while they slept in their $700 silk Bergdorf Goodman pajamas.

Such a moment cannot be allowed, will not be allowed.

The 38th-floor penthouses can shake, the president can shit oyster shells (or broccoli stumps) but we cannot have the supple, outraged, funny, utterly original voice of Bukowski among us. He has committed the grand felony of remaining himself and creating through 40 books a world that doesn't pay the faintest allegiance to anything we've ever been told about civilization.

A biographer who would have even attempted to get past the spurious labels by which the hardback-buying public carves up the earth and buggers it to a standstill, and reconstruct the comic-nightmare world of Bukowski, with all of its fits and starts, bravery and self-destruction and mock bravado, its anguish and small victories its chronically precarious hold on life along with its insistence on not giving in to anything or anybody who is false – such a biographer would have been told in a form letter, "We wish you luck elsewhere." That's what they do up there in New York when you write something that is whole. They wish you luck. This is a euphemism and in reality is saying, "You asshole, don't you see how carved up the world is? Cunts and cocks and mouths and assholes on this side. Delicate and sensitive literary phrasing about the flawed but compassionate stature of man on the other side. Feel free to query us if you have a future manuscript that has a definite market in mind." Yes, darling, the butt-fuckers anonymous of East Orange, New Jersey.

For a biographer to have delved very deeply into the resistance toward Bukowski, to what John Rechy, writing in the *Los Angeles Times,* calls that begrudging of "respectful attention by the tomes that purport to establish literary importance," would have opened a can of maggots. It's not merely, then, that the New York "cultural elite," including Random House, would have been flushed into the open, but the whole gamut of "literary" houses, elite journals and prestigious small press publishers and magazines, wholesalers and distributors would have been set up like wooden ducks in a traveling carny to reveal them for what they are: just wood, and hollow wood at that. Then, once the prevailing and hopeless cultural hypocrisy had been sniffed out, the biographer would have been forced to go back to the work, to truly feel it, and evaluate it to see why Bukowski has so deeply disturbed all levels of the literary pecking order, indeed all of what can be called "respectable" society for the last 40 years.

He would see that much of the tension in Bukowski's work grows out of a fear and rage over the fly caught in the spider's web and the knowledge that life functions mostly in that way – eat or be eaten, Bukowski and all of us as murderers or murdered – unless, as Miller noted, humans can somehow find their way back to their custodial function as intermediaries between nature and the gods, preserving and enhancing what will grow, not die. That takes courage and imagination, and Bukowski has both. In the end it saves him from the vicious cycle of the treadmill that coughs up most people like battered tin cans.

And if the cultural scene is even half as calcified as I say it is, who would have benefited from a true biography of Charles Bukowski? It would benefit the 15- and 20-year-olds who feel lost right now, who in the words of Bukowski's fictional alter ego, Henry Chinaski, says, "Your parents controlled your growing-up period, they pissed all over you. Then, when you got ready to go out on your own, the others wanted to stick you in a uniform so you could get your ass shot off." These young people, at least a handful of them, also might be browsing the library shelves, as Bukowski once did, and perhaps remarking as Bukowski once remarked about books, "It seemed as if everybody was playing word tricks." Then . . . then to discover a book that speaks in true words about a true man and excites the bewildered 15-year-old to say of Bukowski's biographer, as Bukowski once said of John Fante, "And here, at last, was a man who was *not afraid of emotion*." It won't happen, not in our lifetime, and probably never, no more than it happened for Gogol or Céline or Miller or Hamsun or Nathaniel West (W.C. Fields is an exception in having a biographer like Robert Lewis Taylor).

What we have is the work. It's all we ever have. And briefly, what might a 15-year-old think upon discovering Bukowski: Here was a man who found a way not to get hard like the others.

For Bukowski is finally Quasimodo locked in the bell tower of his alcoholic ding-dong, who, without leaving his room, rings the bells of alarm and saves beauty. No, not the beautiful woman, but the indisputable link between truth and beauty that resides in his heart, though he be labeled beast and his crossing the path of ordinary citizens be labeled "bad luck." "Oh that I were stone," Quasimodo cries, wrapped around a stone gargoyle as he watches the mob carry off the beautiful woman he has saved. But the beauty is that he, and Bukowski, haven't become embittered and turned to stone like the rest. As one anonymous and well-heeled coed cried to Bukowski after a reading at Vassar College, "You're so ugly, you're beautiful."

masturbation in the strophe factory: 4 essays on contemporary poetry*

I

This article grew out of a letter sent to George Garrett. It was addressed to his remarks in a long article in the fall issue of The Texas Review *on the current rigor mortis of American Poetry. In the article, about 15 poets addressed Garrett's question: What would they like to see in my future poetry?*

When I first read Garrett I thought here's someone who has finally stuck a darning needle to that Great Blimp in the Combat Zone – American Poetry from 1960–1980. He and the poets interviewed simply said, "Let's cut the crap, start from scratch, be honest and write poetry that has a real need to be written." As I read each poet's comments on what he would like to see happen in American poetry, I readily agreed. The problem came after I had read them all: I couldn't remember one comment from the other. Now, this seems odd in a group as endowed with language and supposedly a desire for the truth as these poets are. Oh, I remembered a few scraps like "funkier language," "greater intensity," "more mature," "closer to the heart," "greater plurality." But I didn't remember anything about the speaker or what he really wanted from poetry. If these poets were editors, would I have a sense of what their magazine was really about? Do I have any sense of them as people who eat, burp, fiddle with their nostril hairs, earn money, screw, and snooze? No, like most of the poems and stories being published, their remarks *seemed* modestly appropriate, modestly interesting, humane, covetously civilized.

---

* Author's note: These essays were written in the early and middle 1980s. Little, if anything, has really changed since then.

No one said, "I'd like to read a poem that would make me laugh my ass off." Humor isn't mentioned at all among the 15 poets though Garrett does refer to "wit". No one said, "I'd like to see some poems with the jaundiced and highfalutin' spirits of W.C. Fields. I'd like to see a poem in the future which makes me want to trip my grandmother. I want some poems about snobbery and folly. I want poems that are infantile, prejudiced, ornery, set in memorable cadences that talk about how manipulation is bred in an American child since the age of two and how that child grows up to run an English department." No one said, "I'd like to see more poems like the kind I write." Well, I would – not the early poems but the kind I've written for the last four years.

A reader might not like the notion of meeting me in H.B. Springer Hall or climbing into the rack with me but dammit there's a hint of personality, a hint of temperament in my comments. And temperament is exactly what contemporary poetry and prose is lacking. The trouble with all the poets Garrett interviewed is that they wouldn't know what to do with "surprising" or "extreme" poetry if they got it. How do I know? Garrett, in discussing corruption in poetry awards, judiciously falls back on the statement, "In the real world we not only draw inferences from actions, we have to do so." Okay, I'll draw inferences from the poets Garrett interviewed and Hayden Carruth, poetry editor of *Harper's* magazine.

More than two years ago Carruth sounded the alarm, saying that a decade that began with so much poetry promise had fizzled into a terrible disappointment. His reasons and evaluations, like Garrett's, were mostly on the mark. Much as Garrett did, he took a hacksaw to what he called "workshop writing" spewing out of the colleges like cans of tuna. It took balls on Carruth's part to challenge the industry he was entrenched in and I told him so. I suggested some areas where he might dig the surgeon's scalpel a little deeper. Then I watched *Harper's*. What would they review? What kind of poems would they print?

Well, they reviewed slush and printed slush. Carruth reviewed Frances Mayes' book and Wendy Salinger's book, both of which are as provocative as a whisk broom. Salinger won one of czar Halpern's National Poetry Competition awards and had been wormed into space on a New York publisher's list. Frances Mayes just happens to run the San Francisco Poetry Forum.

The above are examples of power responding to power. There were a dozen others. The same held true with the poems he's published between 1978–1980.

I challenged Carruth on the above and his response is interesting: "I'm willing to go along with your feeling that I failed . . . I write in a hurry, think in a hurry, and my comments about specific books may seem contradictory because I haven't worded them properly. I have thousands of manuscripts to read – I'm not joking – and that goes with starting a new semester in my new profession, plus an essay of 6,000 words that was due on January 1 . . ."

Hayden Carruth, for all his relative honesty, good intentions, isn't going to change anything at *Harper's*. And it's not because he's corrupt, not in the usual sense of the meaning of that word. He's caught in the numbers game. Like George Garrett and myself and most of the writers across America, he's running, running, running. Some are running for office. Most are just running because that's the nature of American society. If he were here to say to *Harper's*, "Look, this work load is absurd. Get some qualified readers and pay them well because poetry is psychological survival for me and might well be for a few hundred sane souls left out there," then Jimmy Ghost or whoever runs *Harper's* would say to him: "The magazine's on thin sledding. We're lucky to even run poetry. Be happy with what you have. You could be out selling insurance for a living."

A lot of writers have faced the same situation in universities or Poets In The Schools or any number of sponsoring agencies who play all kinds of games with us. The ten-year love affair the government had for American artists has come to an end. It was the kind of love a mother bestows on a child.

It isn't so much what they perpetrate on us as what we allowed to happen to us because we were scared we wouldn't get our cut. Compared to plumbers or lawyers or doctors there is nothing unusual there except writers were running around with a banner over their heads that said, "We got the Truth, Motherfucker." We got all decorous and respectable and self-conscious about our self-anointed priesthood. As I traveled the country harvesting my own cut of the pie (based on eight poems that were acceptable to arts council panels), I heard poets complain about ripoffs in the small press scene, chronic abuse and contract violations in PITS*, and misuse of NEA** funds for college readings and residencies.

Other than Jennifer Moyer, AIS*** coordinator of the Illinois Arts Council, who says the only way she could begin to rid the corruption festering in that state's arts council was to instigate open meetings which the press attended, I don't know of any writers or administrators who made much of a squawk about the wholesale slime that was connected with arts money in the '70s.

Poet David Ray has regularly run editorials decrying the lack of integrity of New York publishing houses. He is noted for his attempts to get PEN to set standards to protect writers. He prides himself on publishing the work of promising new writers. And he should. Once, though, he came up to me after a reading and said both my remarks and poems were "too confrontational." "That won't do you any good at all," he said. I replied that some of the poems had been printed in his magazine *New Letters*, but Ray shook his head as if shaking loose a fly on his eyebrow.

His message was much like that of a former arts coordinator: "You can pretty much do what you want in the classroom

---

*   Poetry in the Schools.
**   National Endowment for the Arts.
*** Artists in the Schools.

but be careful what kind of student writing you send to the newspaper." She was referring to fifth graders' poems about their umbilical cords that roused a Baptist School board out of their real estate offices for an "emergency meeting". The guest poet who perpetrated these umbilical atrocities – David Ray.

One could excuse the "image making" poets on the grounds that in difficult economic times they have to perform numerous and shoddy hustles just to eat and get a little writing done. Didn't Keats have to sneak up and down London alleys late at night snatching little doggies for medical experiments?

But there's a difference between "selling" the idea of poetry and strangling mutts. A casual remark from another "successful" writer Carolyn Osborne (University of Illinois Press, *Paris Review*, *New Letters*, *Antioch Review*) does more to put the difference and the mediocrity of contemporary writing in perspective than all the NEA ripoffs and insidious "cronyism" over the past ten years. After reading two of my stories she said, "I could never write wild stories like this. Nobody would publish me if I did."

In a phrase she tells me what most writers have become: respectable. This explains why they don't buck those sponsoring institutions, why any gathering of them sounds more like probate lawyers hustling for corpses. Though 99.8% of the population wouldn't know Alan Dugan (a lot of poets don't either) or Russell Edson from the spring mechanism on an Atlas rocket, poets scramble and bicker over the fish bones of economics and power. Poets talk about their industry in the same spurious and soporific language doctors and lawyers use to conceal their billion dollar hustles.

When a poet does protest NEA shenanigans, the implications are ironic, if not grim. Take writer and small press editor, Dave Oliphant in Austin, Texas. Quite justifiably he, and others in Texas, complained that their presses were being short-changed while all the spoils went to New York and California (*The Texas Review* has a chart on this at the end of Garrett's article.) Under a barrage of angry letters and telephone calls, many of them Oliphant's, NEA whisked one of its representatives, former magazine editor Mary MacArthur on a plane to Austin where 400 of the faithful (a curiosity in itself since a poetry reading in Austin is lucky to get 50 people) waited in livid curiosity to find out why they weren't getting their cut of the pie. Lovely Mary, as might be expected, delivered a GM speech to the stockholders but many of the stockholders, including Oliphant, didn't buy it.

While Oliphant tried to badger Mary MacArthur out of her euphemisms, I couldn't help smiling. The previous spring I'd listened to Mr. Oliphant address students at the University of Texas as part of an event called Small Presses of Texas Day or some such thing. A student asked: "When you're just starting out, how do you go about getting published?" Oliphant's answer: "You start your own press. You publish your friends. Later, when they get presses they publish you."

This is hardly a recommendation for me or the general public to buy his press's books or his own, especially when you consider that NEA and the Texas Circuit claim they're trying to promote contemporary literature. But Oliphant shouldn't be chided. He was only saying what is in fact going on in every state in this country. I've come to believe that any quality literature that does get published is largely by accident.

Groups forming to protect their identity and special interests are logical enough, except that literature used to be in the business of touching other people. NEA has spent several million dollars for "programs that would reach a wider audience" and that's money that might as well have been dumped in the Grand Canyon for pack mules to munch on. As I've crisscrossed the country, I've talked to a lot of people who weren't writers, who've sampled one or two readings. A few were students; mostly they were people between 25 and 35; they struck me as bright, well-read in fields outside of literature, curious. A handful said they were delighted with the one or two readings they'd attended. The majority said they'd been bored and would not go back for another reading.

The most poignant remark of Garrett's piece is a writer's comment that poets are as much locked into the times as any salesman, doctor, lawyer, or Indian chief. Should we wonder, then, that if the times have become increasingly group centered and the members of each group increasingly monitored, that poets should have the same smugness, hypocrisy, respectability, and dullness as lawyers while offering us a product which, like our meat and soup, is increasingly watered down, loaded with artificials, and spiced with brilliant, vacuous labeling.

Where I differ from Carruth and Garrett and other writers about the literary scene is their contention that the mediocrity has been largely a product of university writing programs and grant-giving programs. Garrett's analysis is far more complex, but I think the failure of the writing in the '60s and '70s goes much deeper. I do not share his optimism about the future of poetry or the poets he interviewed: "As much as each and all seem to be dissatisfied with the present situation, *all* feel that something can and ought to be done about it." (Italics mine.)

Much of my letter to Garrett discussed the above and for reasons of space can't be elaborated here. I don't believe writers are any more rotten than anybody else, just that all of us, particularly college graduates of any profession, have fallen for a tactic designed to keep us peaceful, law-abiding citizens: Discourse Mistaken For Reality.

It is something that began when we were in college and read our Orwell and Huxley and J.D. Salinger, railed righteously against the conformist world, and having found the right attitude, promptly went about the business of collecting the union card though it was a dull, wearisome business day after day sitting passively in a classroom. Sixteen or eighteen or twenty years in school and not much to show for it except the *possibility* that we might eat a little better than our parents did and have a split level in Shaker Heights.

We have become a nation where the right things always get said but very little is done about it. The oil shortage hoax in '73 and '79, the Kennedy and King assassinations; the list is endless. The disease is one which spread from universities to the rest of the country – once having rigorously analyzed a problem, identified its roots, its possible remedies, we get smug and rest assured that the problem will somehow take care of itself.

For many writers, particularly those who've laid a claim stake in the literary power system, the kibitzing and finger-pointing in the industry will suffice to restore a sense of moral rightness. To get off the train and quit running or being run may seem physically impossible to some writers because of commitments to raising a family. Others simply won't make the sacrifice. It would mean trying to find the tools and cultural supports to begin reshaping oneself. It would mean isolation and giving up the old cultural supports on which a false ego has been nurtured for so many years. It would mean undergoing the vertigo that the hero of Carpentier's *The Lost Steps* went through. It would mean loneliness that would drive weaker souls crazy.

A final anecdote. It's about the difficulty of maintaining a friendship with another poet when the other poet decides you're in the way of his literary survival. It's also about the incredible pettiness that characterizes relationships between writers these days. We'll call this fellow Nicolas Kolumban. Aided by a priest, he slipped through some farm fields and escaped from Eastern Europe to the U.S. in the late '50s. We met as undergraduates over a sink as dishwashers in a college fraternity house. We had intense discussions about literature, collegiate conformity, the possibility that we might get laid next week or the week after. We lost track of each other for fifteen years but were reunited at a Sandra McPherson reading in Easton, Pennsylvania. Nicolas Kolumban's got a shrewd peasant's sense of earthiness, loves a good joke, and is utterly unaffected. But . . . he decided to get into the small press business. He started a magazine. He took a poem of mine, held it for a year, then called me one Sunday to say he wasn't going to print it. It had the word "fag" in it, used ironically. Kolumban thought there was a certain member of the NEA grants for magazines panel who might object to the use of the word "fag". He had applied for a grant for the ailing magazine.

It wasn't just that I objected to a friend doing his hustle at my expense and a poem I had worked on for weeks to get right. It was more the feeling, "Oh no, not another one." Another one gone the way of a pettiness bordering on pathos where there was so little to be gained.

If ever there was a time when the lines from Yeats' poem made sense, it is now: *The best lack all conviction, while the worst are full of passionate intensity.*

II

"Workers usually make the mistake of wanting to be regarded as respectable citizens, but no one thinks the better of them for it."
B. Traven, *The Cottonpickers*

Poets for the last 30 years in America have not been much different than stockbrokers, psychologists, PR men, CPAs*, suburban Methodist preachers, computer analysts, lawyers, doctors, and telephone company executives. Like their young urban professional counterparts, sometimes known as YUPPIES, their product is understood only by their own members; indeed, it was designed that way. The language between the doctor and the pharmacist is meant to be understood by nobody but themselves, though they do not drink the magic potion. It's the same with poets. Their jargon and non-talk insulates their elitism and protects them from scrutiny. True, they have few patients except a group of neurotic kids flocking to the writing programs but like other professionals they have been educated to mystify their work, to keep it tidy, obscure, and formal. George Garrett, in an article for *The Texas*

---

* Certified Public Accountants.

Review, has said the more successful poets carry themselves "like priests."

Most lesser ones do it too. Their demeanor is grave, they seldom look healthy; the words are pronounced as if they were marbles rolling off a table. They are offering us ART. If the words rarely touch a nerve in us, a sense of recognition, that's because poets have become modest little technicians, not even relevant to themselves.

Here are some other traits shared by contemporary American poets and YUPPIES: a marvelous ability to reduce human conflict to comfortable, hollow notions; an utter lack of courage when confronting authority; little understanding or curiosity about America's role in world history; a curious deafness of tone; a detachment from their bodies both in person and in their work. The so-called professional poet is so sexless as to raise the question what he's doing on earth at all. Maxine Hong Kingston would have called them "ghosts." These ghosts scurry about with an air of self-importance, though any scrutiny reveals them to be ill at ease. They have little interest in a community except an intramural one that will further solidify their privileged position. The closer you get to the big cities, the higher you climb the professional ladder of success, the more you find a climate of "Every man for himself," a Darwinian orgy of sadism, self-flagellation, and rigidity.

Poets view chicanery, manipulation, and duplicity as a way of life yet they are quick to condemn any act or person that strikes their specious morality as criminal. Violence is rejected, regardless of the situation, as a way of dealing with injustice. In short, you have in the American poet a person with the moral rigor of a Rotarian grain buyer, yet one whose evasiveness abets a society built on violence and hypocrisy. He is as institutionalized as a man who has spent his entire adult life in a maximum security prison.

Randall Jarrell's comment about how poets lost audiences and inherited classrooms after World War II is well-known.

What is forgotten are the implications of the date: 1945. This is the year America began to move into the gap left by the depleted European nations and exploit the earth to supply luxuries a new middle class demanded. The process was very similar to Rome, systematically crushing the cultures of its neighbors which had for several centuries served as a buffer between the barbarians and the heart of the empire.

America was the barbarian after World War II. Unlike previous tyrants, it did not care if the Indian or black man kissed the Cross (though Christianity could be useful in completing enslavement) or swore subservience to The Empire, or adopted the language of the masters. Much of the American Empire had already been built by slaves (black and white) and, unlike the French, it was seen as a disadvantage to have slaves around who could read or write. Anyway, America had only one culture to export and that was the desire for profit. It did not want the slave's soul, just his bauxite, oil, his fields bearing that one crop that Wall Street said would bring a good price that particular year.

1945 was the year the final brickwork of the old colonialism crumbled. As early as 1913, Ambassador Page had written to Woodrow Wilson: "The future of the world belongs to us. . . . Now what are we going to do with the leadership of the world presently when it falls into our hands?" That "leadership," says Aimé Césaire, a poet from Martinique, not only mechanized man but completed "the gigantic rape of everything intimate."

As the Empire has grown and progressive wealth has been exported to America, the rich in the form of their foundation and museum lackeys, universities and arts councils have felt a greater and greater need to validate their exploitation. They want something called ART to prove they are "civilized" after all. This "Art" is the final dash of color, form, line, whatever technical jargon you want to use, to rationalize your room built upon skeletons.

There is no room for anything with real intimacy, content, boldness. It is too much for our senses which have been taught to see art as a subtle, civilizing maneuver. We do not need censorship; we censored ourselves long ago. The proof is this article. It will not excite any more comment, let alone action, than a man buttoning his fly at Times Square. In America everything is permitted and nothing taken seriously. In artsy circles it is considered bad manners to get excited about anything. Words themselves have become so inflated as to be little more than time-fillers till we find out who can be useful to our sad, little hustle. There is a feeling that all has been said, yet nothing came of it so it is not a matter of the rage in this article; rage and impotency are reflected in every other face on the street. A handful of people celebrate what there is to celebrate, which is still considerable – a young woman singing arias in a subway passage while the sultry mob surges around her, grimfaced as usual; a young go-getter in his Gimbel's wash 'n' wear suit and handsome briefcase raises his index finger to his temple and makes the screwball sign. Our poets will not be witness to any of this, not the breakdown, nor the joy of the courageous few.

It's not that I would have them go to El Salvador via Carolyn Forché and detail the bodies in the town dump. Forché's poems on that country are affected, condescending little set pieces and show what happens when an American poet tries to overlay his education in technical subtleties with an atrocity. You get a crash course in slumming.

No, I would have poets take seriously what Baudelaire wrote: "Everything in this world reeks of crime: the newspaper, the wall, the countenance of man."

By knowing what to say "No" to, they could then discover those eyes, hands, artichokes, cafés, loins, and screwdrivers that deserve their resounding "Yes." It is precisely American poets' inability to identify the enemy that makes their poetry so mediocre. Instead, they have worn the mantle of the outsider, the priest, the defeated without realizing that writing is a privilege taken mainly by stealth; and, in the words of Victor

Serge, "no one is ever really outside society." The notion of the suffering poet in his garret is little more than a romantic myth perpetuated by art's hucksters. The bourgeoisie love that mythology as long as they don't have to get too close to the messiness of art. Poets have cooperated in recent years by cleaning up their act, by being respectable little citizens as they paraded to the podium, yet hinting that their wares came from untold privation and suffering. Such "artists" have a literary ego but no real ego and anybody with true well-being, any real gusto for life, will by virtue of his mere appearance among them find himself singled out as The Enemy.

Balzac and Stendahl, among others, have detailed the process of the above paragraph. In *Lost Illusions*, Balzac has Lousteau tell the budding poet Lucien, "The key to success in literature is not to work oneself but to exploit other's work. . . . The more mediocre a man is, the sooner he arrives at success; he can swallow insults, put up with anything, flatter the mean and petty passions of the literary sultans . . ."

Luis Buñuel put American literary history in perspective when he said, "It seems clear to me that without the enormous influence of the canon of American culture, Steinbeck would be unknown, as would Dos Passos and Hemingway. If they'd been born in Paraguay or Turkey, no one would ever have read them, which suggests the alarming fact that the greatness of a writer is in direct proportion to the power of his country. Galdos, for instance, is often as remarkable as Dostoevsky, but who outside Spain ever reads him?"

It is not merely the power of a given country but to what uses they can put foreign writers. Solzhenitsyn is given large press but who knows that the contemporary Voinovich is an infinitely better writer? Or for that matter other Soviet writers who were not officially sanctioned in the old USSR – Alexander Herzen; Vissarion Belinsky, whose literary criticism if taken seriously by American critics would result in a whole new look at our writing; Victor Serge, political historian and novelist.

The Peruvian poet Vallejo's work was well-known by Spanish and European poets in the '30s. Why did it take 40 years before his brilliant, somber poems reached American poets?

Why in the recent "boom" of Latin American writers is the Cuban novelist Alejo Carpentier seldom mentioned except by Hispanic writers?

The list could go on and on about a body of writing with a greater variety and feeling for the truth than American culture offers. I am forced to conclude that Buñuel is right: American books are found throughout the world, not because they are the best that can be offered, or are even good, but because it's a dying Empire's abortive effort to prove that it is, after all, civilized.

The Mailers, Updikes, Bellows do not challenge the systems which give them their preeminence. They are held up as cultural ideals but their work has no center of feeling or thought and more important, little sense of surprise. Typical of American writing, these esteemed artists muddle in a moral anarchy rather than clarifying it. In interviews they would make us think otherwise but their own writing, for all its dabbling in ideas, finally reinforces the American cultural norm: there are no ideas worth taking seriously.

Despite the fact that one-half the population has gone to college, where they all get at least a semester of exposure to literature, most Americans still think of serious writing in the context of "ivory tower", "romantic", "effete", and above all, Intellectual. These terms may be unjust, given a certain variety in American fiction and poetry during the last 40 years, but they have a very real basis. The tradition of fiction and poetry in most of the world, particularly outside Western Europe, has not only cast deep suspicion on the powerful and rich but reveals a consistent interest in the lives of the marginal, the oppressed, the mad, the eccentric, the poor. Except in America. John Kenneth Galbraith's comment about our best writers' attitude toward the rich summarizes fiction but the inferences drawn from it can easily be applied to poets: "In the late 1920s and the years of the great flowering of American fiction there was a major change in the treatment of the rich: they ceased to be socially offensive or economically exploitative and became positively benign. Now it was *their* problems that attracted attention. This, perhaps surprisingly, continued to be true in the Depression years of the '30s, *The Grapes of Wrath* being something of an exception, as also the earlier novels of John Dos Passos."

How interesting that this comment comes from someone outside the literary camp.

The term "rich" is bound tight with another word, "respectability." In a country where there has not been the cultural and historical division of classes as there has been in other countries, writers have often shopped in both camps of the rich and the marginal, using language both respectable (tactful they might say) and blunt. Mark Twain–Samuel Clemens may have originated American vernacular but he also started the "business" of the artist kowtowing to respectability when he allowed his wife to delete any words she thought offensive in *Huckleberry Finn*. His schizophrenia of wanting to play ball in two opposed camps is at the heart of American writers' ultimate loneliness and desperation. I've always found it amusing that Twain is held up as an example of a satirist.

Even more amusing in the last twenty years is the obsession of American poets, bordering on a mania, for respectability. Since no one is listening to them, not the government, nor any audience even approaching an intellectual body, nor the literate masses, I find this mania pathetically comic. I can think of no more deluded or sadder group in this country.

Both writers and audiences began at the same place: until the age of two we were taught to walk and talk; after the age of two we were told to shut up and sit down. Fifty years later, most Americans are still sitting down and shutting up. This is what makes a "great" technological power able to exercise political power in Chile, economic power in Central America, dominance over seven tenths of the world. Indeed, the former slave countries of Ireland and St. Lucia in the West Indies, for all their misery, strike me as considerably freer in their expression than this dominant country of technocrats.

I think of part of the definition of a poet as someone who feels more deeply and sees more clearly so as to be able to show his country how to see more clearly. To do this he would have to rebel at some point against this shut up and sit down dictum. Judging by most of the poetry written, such rebellion has never taken place. They have been busy being "good" little boys and girls. A more honest profession would have been as pimps at 23rd and 10th in New York. But the illusion that they are professionals in "art" persists, and the arts councils and universities aid them in this myopia.

Eight years ago Edward Albee told a Bucknell University audience, "You people don't want the truth; you just want to be entertained." The repressive backlash from the '60s gets more constraining each year on university campuses. Yet they continue to make room for more poets, more workshops, more conferences. Poets cooperate in this relatively new business hustle by essentially being passive. If they told those middle-class twits, not sure what to do with their lives, the truth, the kids would take up data processing. But the poet, himself, long ago has learned the same game his students have – SHUT UP AND SIT DOWN. As he gets older, our poet learns that the rules don't change, just the title for them. He must wait for authority before he marches to recess. He must pare his wildness, enthusiasm, anger, sense of misgiving, sadness to manageable proportions. Above all he must learn the lesson so obvious at every level of American society – people don't count, just your superiors. Much of this our little poet has learned by junior high school. Only now it is called DON'T MAKE A MISTAKE.

"You make one mistake and you're out," is what an arts

administrator told me when I went to Texas in 1977 to do poetry-in-the-schools work. She liked the idea of kids getting "art" and her own notion of art was largely taken from Bach and medieval art. I doubt she was aware of Benvenuto Cellini and the absolute war it took to produce "pretty" vases; in other words her idea was that art should be "decorative". This woman is a distinct and recurring type found in arts bureaucracies and the type is not there by accident. Like our Yuppies, the poet and his pal, the arts administrator, all hold hands down a primrose path strewn with pleasant diversion. Struggle must be eliminated if the machine gears are to roll smoothly and those who insist on any sort of struggle are violating DON'T MAKE A MISTAKE.

Naomi Lazzard made a mistake even considering doing an article commissioned by *Harper's* on "the poetry mafia," a comical misnomer in itself. Carolyn Kizer told her so; so did "a number of other prominent poets." They told her she'd "be finished in poetry," if she did such an article. Various arts councils and universities pooled their resources and bought her a bottle of liquid soap and as of this writing she is blowing bubbles in various MFA* programs around the country. Everyone considers her a success. To be a success is to be respectable. Wherever you are reading this, stand up and applaud the success of Naomi and Carolyn and wee Richie Howard and Uncle Kunitz and all the other poet successes quietly sitting at the front of Mrs. Diefenbacher's fifth grade class, quietly polishing their apples.

Those writers who do not go along with the party line get fired, and sometimes so do their friends. It goes on all the time in the American Yuppie scene and in economic terms it's called "carom screwing". The ironies pile over each other with the speed of a Marx Brothers movie. The demand for instant success insists on a language that is both specious and cautious. Everyone, everyone must obey the party line. But in a theoretical democracy, no one is quite sure what the party

---

* Master of Fine Arts.

line is, so the scramble becomes more and more insane each year. A single poem can have four or five contradictory messages. Yes, there is an easy workshop writing going on, born of casual metaphor but poets' failure to find out what they really feel and think makes them subject themselves to psychotic splits and we get a poetry utterly without clarity. Their struggle is not a real struggle; their voices are those of men and women who write out of habit but no conviction. Some editors complain of the lack of humor in poets but that's because they have never struggled for anything beyond success. Mayakovsky committed suicide after writing poems for the new-line Bolshevik regime which squashed all freedom in Russia. American poets don't have that kind of courage; they commit a slow suicide because unwittingly they speak in the interests of repression. They hark back to Whitman and Eliot but show me one that even approaches Whitman's buoyancy or Eliot's critical powers. Poetry in the States operates in a vacuum where history is discarded and poets become the sycophantic clerks their fathers were.

III

"The mere fact that the younger American literary generation has come to the schools instead of running away from them is an indication of a soberer and less coltish spirit."

Wallace Stegner, Stanford University,
Creative Writing Program

W.D. Snodgrass, in his foreword to *Dance Script with Electric Ballerina* by Alice Fulton, the Associated Writing Programs' award co-winner this year in poetry, explains a disease which has run rampant for so long it now feels ancient, not merely with AWP, but with other prizes as well: "On every side manuscripts appear, with high praise, exactly like seven other volumes one has read that year; if you accidentally dropped and scrambled all eight manuscripts, not even the authors could tell. In place of real talent, energy, passion, one sees poem after poem" (or story after story) "written to fit the fashion, the political or literary movement of the week, the needs of 1,000 half-dead graduate students, the obsession and power-hungry theories of critic A or B."

Like other able critics of the shriveled literary spirit in recent years, Mr. Snodgrass sees clearly the symptoms but not that he and a few thousand other writing teachers are part of the cause. If he were to say to those "half-dead graduate students" who show up in classes, "You're half-dead because you've been hanging around school for the last 17 years. The first assignment in this course will be to get out of here and take a job as a checkout clerk at Woolworth's," Mr. Snodgrass would be thrown out of his warm stall and forced to join his creative writing majors at the five-and-dime, or the unemployment line.

AWP is AWP because creative writing programs have blossomed ten-fold in the last thirteen years and this could not have happened if more than a thimble's worth of critical spirit or life had seeped into the classroom. It's so much easier to do metaphor exercises, character sketches, and study line breaks than talk about the expansiveness of James Wright or Whitman or why Robert Penn Warren makes the statement, "there's a lot of talent out there but not much fire." Students are satisfied they're getting something tangible; their basic sense of comfort hasn't been tampered with. As long as you're locked in "workshop exercises" everyone has hope and pays their money for the next term. The writing teacher hasn't said anything controversial or defeating; the deans haven't had to deal with anything messier than a writing instructor screwing an occasional student; the English Department chairman is satisfied something like "real discipline" and not "a bull session" is going on in your classroom. At the AWP convention in San Antonio in 1980 I listened to several writing teachers whine about the "prize-winning" poems and stories that had just been read by the proud authors. But none of them whined where it could be heard. It would have been bad for business.

Umberto Eco, touring America this year, compared humanities departments to prisons. They have no relationship with the community. This would be unthinkable in Italy, he said. When you add to this claustrophobia the pettiness and hypocrisy of the American university, is it any surprise that its products have as much relevance to people's struggles as a pound of oleomargarine? But the creative writing boys such as Mr. Snodgrass would have us see them as mavericks within the system.

If the young writer needs an instructive example of the meanness and pettiness and utter disregard for talent with which many universities treat the writer who tries to go his own way, he could do no better than a biography on Theodore Roethke called *The Glass House*. Can anyone imagine an American university printing a Gorky, Nathaniel West, Rabelais, or Nelson Algren?

What we have as a fiction prizewinner is *Delta Q*, by Alvin Greenberg. The collection was chosen by Ted Solotaroff from approximately 200 submissions. Solotaroff is an editor of "serious" fiction at Harper & Row and his choice tells us something about the diminishing distance between large and small presses. Solotaroff does not offer us a Foreword explaining his selection but if the title and rarified tone of the stories bewilder us, the back cover offers us enlightenment: "Just as the Heisenberg Uncertainty Principle, from which the title is drawn, postulates a limit to the accuracy with which science can observe and describe the universe, so Greenberg examines man's perplexity at the discovery that human knowledge is limited."

Greenberg's first examination centers around some pigs. Their lead sow scratches the word LOVE in the dirt. This leads the nameless narrator, a writer – what else – to some ruminations about what pigs have done to a library: "Whole books, my own among them, are missing. I am not sure how to account for this, but it makes little difference; there is enough reading material here to last a lifetime, and besides, are we not now in the very process of developing an entire community of writers on this island? Soon, soon, I hope I will be able to begin reading them."

Mr. Greenberg will have access to them sooner than he thinks because as he knows they are *group*, and as *group* they will be quick to imitate the nation's prizewinners, including Mr. Greenberg.

Greenberg's stories feed solely on interpretation; the dissertation folks at MLA would have a field day with them. Many of them are monologues by narrators without names, without a neighborhood, without an odor, with the energy of a sloth just after feeding time. What they do offer is a muted, cautious irony like a blinking yellow light to remind us life is a remote snicker. This irony is about so little that I finally suspect that the joke is on Greenberg. He doesn't have very much to write about except writing and literature, as the following titles indicate: "The Power of Language," "To Be or Not to Be," "Disorder and Belated Sorrow," "Not a Story by Isaac Bashevis Singer," "Who Is This Man and What Is He Doing in My Life?" Should The Club members complain this year about the quality of the prizewinners, Greenberg can tell them, "Some pigs are more equal than others."

In citing the virtues of Alice Fulton's award-winning book, Snodgrass says, "Her life seems to have been a succession of dances, dancers, performers, costume." I wouldn't quarrel with this. There is great color, movement, and dazzlement in this poetry. Almost every line is a blazing light show. That is the way Fulton would have it: "You've seen kids on Independence Day, waving/sparklers to sketch their initials on the night?/ Just so, I'd like to leave a residue/ of slash and glide, a trace/ form on the riled air."

But sparklers fizzle very quickly; to keep up the illusion that something real is going on, you have to light them faster and faster to convince the crowd this day was worth celebrating. The search for independence gets lost in the fireworks display.

In discussing her own buoyancy, Ms. Fulton says, "I didn't create this painful grace./ I didn't banish the primitive." After reading these poems several times I feel this is exactly what she has done. She is so conscious of the clever turn of phrase that she consistently outfinesses her subject. The primitive has been banished; there is a grace to these poems; but it is not of the "painful" variety.

About her tendency to out-finesse her subject, Snodgrass says, "It may be that at times the fancy footwork obscures the overall shape of the dance – which is to say, I suppose, that she has not quite decided whether she is a poet of style, like Cummings or Berryman, or a poet of subject, like Hardy or Frost."

Such subdivisions by Snodgrass are a lot of nonsense and go a long way toward explaining why we have several hundred cute poets getting prizes for stringing together snazzy images. It explains why 90 percent of the poetry today is inaccessible to anybody but other poets. Style grows out of character and character is our response to the pressures of life. You can relay those pressures in a light manner or a solemn manner or any combination of the two but if you're not deeply involved with your subject matter you get sparkler writing on the air. In citing Pound, Snodgrass calls it "the dance of the intellect" to describe Ms. Fulton's work.

This "dance of the intellect" looks to me like a lot of running in place. There is the illusion of motion but no real movement except in three or four poems where the writer lets other people speak. I have no more sense of knowing the poet here than I would a man running for comptroller with whom I'd spent three hours. Language as a smokescreen. Perhaps this is what Snodgrass means by "the dance of the intellect."

The proliferation of the mediocre is not really news. Imitative dullness, cowardliness, modest aspiration, and lack of a real voice have dominated the daily skirmishes of most literary ages. Balzac documented the literary scene in 1820 in France; Orwell alluded to its corruption often in essays, letters, and book reviews. What is fascinating is the process by which mediocrity gets called art, be it Raymond Carver or in this case some university award winners. In Balzac's time, if a reviewer wanted to pan a book he said "it is the finest the period has produced." That was said about all books, language inflated to say nothing at all. Now we resort to euphemisms that actually amount to an "intellectual dance."

As to why we are offered so much colored dish water that's labeled DRINKABLE, Pablo Neruda says it best: "The bourgeoisie demands a poetry that is more and more isolated from reality. The poet who knows how to call a spade a spade is dangerous to capitalism on its last legs." Capitalism, or Socialism for the Rich, the point is that poems should match the handsome bookcases full of culture which we all know begins with a hush. By its harshness or playfulness, celebration or disdain, a book of poems or stories must not jar the prevailing quiet of the institution that sponsors it. The result is Understatement as a Fetish by Spanky and Our Gang.

When a writer does choose to do a little spade-calling, the process of voluntary censorship to which they allude is fascinating for its implications. In 1981 *Poets & Writers* interviewed Naomi Lazard on a subject called the "poetry mafia." Ms. Lazard said she'd been asked by *Harper's* to do an article about the "poetry mafia." "She wanted very much to do it," the article says. "I was told by several people – including Carolyn Kizer – that if I did it, I'd be 'finished in poetry.'" It's irrelevant whether there's some lyric rhapsodizers toting bean shooters labeled "a poetry mafia"; the attitude of sycophancy and knuckling under make "the family" unnecessary. The knowing Ms. Kizer labeled John "The Whisperer" Ashbery and Harold "Two Knuckles" Bloom as some of the leaders of this "mafia," which shows how little it takes to make the literary crowd tinkle in their boots.

The reward for being a quiet little poet, according to Kizer,

94

is "power" which is "who gets listened to and who doesn't." Since 90 percent of the audience is centered around colleges, poets are fighting over a podium in front of fifty metaphor-logged creative writing students, a glass of sherry, and a chance to admire the dean's wife's new henna hairdo. The lesser colleges offer the visiting writer the chemistry room where he can spot the foreheads of his audience just over the top of the Bunsen burners. Then, if your writing is judged harmless enough for five consecutive years, you get a two-week paid vacation at the Bread Loaf Writers' Conference where, as Gene Lyons reported for *Harper's*, a Vietnam veteran reading from his war experiences was enough to make the veterans of quietude scamper from the carpeted room, mumbling, "Taste! What's become of taste!"

This quietude is what *The New York Times* called "the agony and ecstasy at what is generally considered the best authors' course in the United States – the Iowa University Writers' Workshop." Iowa was not only in on the ground floor of writing programs but of a university prize (actually furnished by the Iowa Arts Council, which is an amazing entity itself) for short stories, presumably like these AWP prizes, making up for the New York publishing houses' lack of interest in the short story or serious writing in general. They were so serious about this prize one year in the mid-70s, they hired a writer named Henderson to screen almost 300 short story manuscripts by himself. They gave him a thousand dollars and three months to boil these submissions down to twenty finalists. Henderson's job was not made easier by the fact that he isn't American. He's from New Zealand and this was his first visit to the States. What he would have done with the idiom of a Richard Wright or a Flannery O'Connor I don't know. But Henderson had his own idiosyncratic approach to such servitude. If the type on the first page was light, he threw it in the rejected pile, he later told me. If the first page of the first story didn't engage him, that manuscript too plopped with the rejects. His advice to me: "If you ever submit to the Iowa contest, buy a new typewriter ribbon first."

My information is that last year's Walt Whitman contest (Academy of American Poets) did employ three screeners to handle several hundred poetry manuscripts. Two of them were MFA students; the third was a young man who said he needed a job. Eric Staley, head of AWP, assures me that for his contests there were four screeners, "each with a published book." However many, it may not be enough to assuage the prevailing feeling among writers that these contests aren't much more than a lottery system. The sponsors no doubt would say there just isn't enough money to pay strong screeners, yet it is curious how universities can always come up with a spare thousand when a "star" writer calls for a reading. Finally, if the two books reviewed here are even among the best, it may not matter how many screeners contests employ or how much they pay them, and writers would be better off investing their time, entry fees, and postage on the weekly lotto.

So why is the postman burdened each week of each year with thousands of manuscripts if writers are fed up with the system? "The only way to get any attention is to win a prize," Greg Kuzma, a Nebraska poet, advises me. Each year, then, we have more and more writers listening to teachers they don't believe, submitting to contests they don't believe in, all so the magic ball with their number on it will be plucked from the wire cage and they will be able to coast for a few years, passing judgment on students and getting paid for it.

Even the normally soft, and sometimes downright syco-phantic, *New York Times Book Review* is getting hip to the dreariness of it all. Says David Bromwich (of Princeton) about W.S. Merwin's latest book, "Mr. Merwin has all the equipment of a poet, but for the moment appears to write from habit rather than impulse . . ." This phrase could describe 90 percent of the poetry and 70 percent of the so-called "serious" fiction published within the last ten years. And Merwin is one of the "stars" who wander in and out of classrooms, advising students.

Heads of creative writing programs are reluctant to tamper with this "star" system even though their students would get more for their money if the head would take the time to find out which writers can write and which writers bring imagination and critical penetration to a workshop. As one writing head explained to me, "No one comes to a reading if the writer's unknown." At the same time, the "stars" know they have nothing to lose by a sodden performance; it will not affect future bookings.

In 1971, the University of West Virginia hired Norman Mailer to spend two hours with its students at a cost of $3,800. For an hour and forty-five minutes of that time, Mailer showed two of his movies and they were dull indeed. When I complained to Mailer by letter saying students deserved better for their money, he wrote back a generous letter, apologizing and explaining that he had been behind in his alimony payments and had to give ten appearances in nine days. This attitude isn't exceptional. Judging by the quality of their readings or addresses, most stars know the university is an easy udder to milk. But the faculty committees and writing programs will go on playing the game because they know damn well the rules of the game do not include the student voice. They are on safe ground – much of the time students are happy to have glimpsed a star whether he has said anything arresting or not.

If this were just a little game played out in colleges, it wouldn't be worth my time addressing. But when you consider that most students arrive at college hating both writing and any reading which challenges their preconceptions, the situation is hypocritical and pathetic. The university is the one institution capable of reversing the situation before young people get funneled into society. Yet its writing programs at every level echo the dreariness and rigidity of the American public school, for reasons just touched on here.

According to Ed Ochester, head of the creative writing program at Pitt, as well as overseer of the Drue Heinz Prize, the Agnes Lynch Starrett Award (for a first book of poetry), and the University of Pittsburgh Press, a committee of faculty and deans must approve visiting writers. Their criteria: 1. the writer must not be politically controversial nor be likely to read politically volatile work; 2. the writer should not be likely to try and seduce faculty wives or students. I don't think Pitt is unusual in this respect.

In discussing university writing programs, Nelson Algren once wrote, "A dedication to the printed word may conceal an indifference toward cruelty; and that understanding of justice and human dignity becomes enfeebled in proportion to one's sophistication should be obvious by now. Unless we've forgotten that it was scholars well-disciplined in Shakespeare, Hegel, Goethe, Freud, Marx, Dante, and Darwin, who yet devised the cultural programs at Auschwitz."

I have my own small experience with a university's obliviousness to injustice or cruelty. Two-and-a-half years ago I wrote to Eric Staley, then editor of the *Missouri Review*, now head of AWP, proposing an essay which dealt with what I considered low-handed tactics by the Missouri Arts Council on writers it sent to schools. His response: "The current genre divisions of the magazine, however, do not seem appropriate to such an essay (they are poetry, fiction, literary criticism, interview, omnibus review). I think the situation is such that the staff would 'worry' about that one when it came up." It used to be called "Protecting my ass," but rarely do you get one of the literary fellas to admit as much. So on top of all this erudite nonsense you get an industry that's stone humorless.

I often associate the word "writer" with "complaining" and most of the complaints listed in this review I've heard from writers at one time or another. But they complain among themselves, never to the appropriate sponsor. As to why this happens, Algren, from the previously quoted essay (which no magazine would print), is best qualified to speak: "Writers bespeak a readiness to be cowed in return for a stall in the Establishment Barn; at whatever cost of originality.

They will not buck. They will not roar. At times they may whimper a bit, softly and just to themselves; but even that they will do quietly."

As visiting writer to the Rocky Mountain Writers Conference in 1968, Algren bombarded his students with water balloons from the roof of his motel. If creative writing programs have to go on, I can think of no better way to begin a class. A truly ambitious program would follow up on this. It would schedule writing classes in a shower room and turn the water on full blast. True, the ink would run but our society is short of competent plumbers, electricians, roofing installers, and auto mechanics.

IV

With hysteria bubbling over about restrictions on the National Endowment for the Arts for 1990-91, perhaps writers will now sit down and take a good look at their own institutions including magazines and reading series, reviewing and trade magazines, prize granting, bookstores – the whole damned lot. From top to bottom, from McMurtry and Keillor (defenders of NEA) to those still unpublished writers, I want them to ask themselves one question: How have we censored ourselves? Until they ask this question, writers are just little urchins standing alongside the road with their hands out, waiting for a sugar-daddy to round them into shape.

From 1972 until 1985 I worked in all sorts of writerly programs, many of them funded by NEA. I am grateful for the chance to have observed how art for thousands of children was not just a bland goodie dumped on them after geography class and just before football practice, but part of their joyous, surging bone marrow.

My God, the stuff they wrote – elated, terrible, funny, sad, and unpredictable. They changed not just the way I thought about writing but about life: We are all born to create; it is that simple and if we don't create, we die. At night, during formally arranged meetings of the PTA, or informally in restaurants and bars, I met these kids' parents and passed out copies of that day's work, and the parents instinctively understood that something valuable was going on. It was a little better to work in the Midwest and Southwest and Plains States than the two coasts, but on the whole, dozens of community organizations gave rich support to children's art.

But a poison was seeping in, surreptitiously at first. Now it is blatant and open. Jesse Helms (who wanted to eliminate the NEA) and we artists of the United States deserve each other. We are much closer than any of you have even begun to guess.

To put the whole business in statistical perspective, arts administration was the second fastest-growing curriculum (next to business administration) in the U.S. during the '70s. From the NEA's inception in 1967 up until 1976, there was a real pioneering spirit because arts programs, like Czechoslovakia in 1990, was run by amateurs. The term "professional writer" reared its head about the same time the phrase "professional arts administrator" seeped in.

The very popularity of arts programs made the administrator and the artist see that art could be used for all sorts of ends that had nothing to do with creation itself. The right image could create a constituency, and in a very young country (as Mr. McMurtry has noted), still fumbling for a moral and cultural base, only a constituency could ensure survival.

There were numerous able arts administrators but usually they were fired by states' arts councils for "not sufficiently promoting arts programs." Like all aspects of today's American society, art was not allowed to progress at its own pace. It had to be pumped, perpetually inflated, constantly sold to some dubious community down the road, always with the right image in mind. It was bonanza time once again at John Sutter's mill, and now we are choking on the poisonous residue of that mineral processing.

Caution and safety were the passwords to artistic success in the '80s. Gold is not what you make but the connections you make. To make the right connections, you need the right image.

An arts administrator (or department chairman, head of a reading series, editor of a magazine, manager of a bookstore, the head of distribution) cannot attract further funding if he has a controversial artist performing down the road at Potsawamie High. The administrator might even admire the teaching and writing of that artist, but he knows he has to ferret him out because he's not good for business.

The line for what was controversial got thinner and thinner. A poet might legitimately be drummed out of a program, as happened in Massachusetts, for screaming "Fuck!" over and over at a group of third graders (ostensibly to prove that words were only words and could be defused by repeating them often enough). But a poet could also quietly be waltzed out of a program for asking a teacher not to read the newspaper in front of the class while the poet was conducting a workshop, as happened in Pennsylvania. If the teacher happened to be the relative of a high-ranking state official, that official could get on the phone with the state arts council and state politicians and list dozens of infractions the poet had perpetrated, even though just a year before the official's relative had written an assessment of this same poet recommending that he return to her fifth graders.

The year was 1978. The poet was canned by the literature panel of the Pennsylvania Arts Council in a note that went, "It is generally not the policy of the Council to employ artists from out of state." However, the National Endowment for the Arts wrote the poet, "Where federal monies are involved, local arts councils cannot disqualify an artist on the grounds of geographical location." But when the NEA sent two representatives to Harrisburg to investigate the matter, they concluded: "We have spent the entire day investigating the files of the Pennsylvania Council on the Arts and can find nothing out of the ordinary in regard to their handling of their situation with your employment."

Enter Texas Senator Lloyd Bentsen who requested a meeting with NEA and claims in a letter that two phone calls and a note went unanswered. A number of now prominent poets worked at that time in Pennsylvania Poets-in-the-Schools. None questioned their employer's decision, though they had worked with the poet for three years, drank beer with him, shared meals in his own home.

Such an example of injustice and betrayal is typical. Although I've used the Poets-in-the-Schools programs as an example, it illustrates the dominant ethic among artists during this period: Stay cool, don't get involved; if another poet gets his ass in a sling, that's his problem.

All during my travels, I heard similar stories like the one involving Pennsylvania. I never heard a story of artists banding together to protect or at least get a fair hearing for one of their fellow artists when an institution decided to yank him around.

When I first went to Texas to work in a Poets-in-the-Schools program, an artist told me, "These programs are always in chaos. The only attitude you can take is what another painter told me: 'Just get the money and run.' Hassles won't get you anywhere."

Given the above, it is no accident that one of the two poets summoned to defend NEA before its critics on the National Council on the Arts in 1990 was Ed Hirsch, who railed at Joseph Epstein's suggestion that Hirsch and his like were "pampered."

So I find it ironic that so many writers are stepping forth now to defend the NEA, like children stripped of their favorite playground when all along they have never viewed the institutions that sponsored them as their institutions but as a benevolent daddy who had come along to help them at the right time. If the Poets-in-the-Schools programs did not work out, they could always hope to get a prize for a book, take up a new and perhaps less vulnerable sanctuary as a writer-in-residence at some college, or if luck was with them, on the tenure track in some MFA program. That so few artists have seen these institutions – publicly funded arts programs as well as universities, journals, bookstores, indeed the very streets, as *theirs*, explains why Robert Penn Warren could say, in response to a *Life* magazine reporter's question, "There's a lot of talent out there but not much fire."

How can you have any fire in your writing when you are unwilling to respond to the oppressiveness of your own institutions, let alone the chronic waste and injustice of a theoretical democracy? To have any fire in your writing, or your life, would be bad for business. Jesse Helms is in the business of playing up to his constituents and getting reelected. As with most other matters, there are no principles at stake in the Congress. It is expediency. Just as it is expediency that governs the thinking of all those writers signing petitions on behalf of the life of the National Endowment for the Arts. It seems the moral thing to do, and none of the biggies want to be thought slack on a matter which could diminish their considerable constituencies.

Where were Susan Sontag and Arthur Miller and E.L. Doctorow and all the rest when the chain bookstores began telling smaller publishers that they had to do a million dollars worth of business with them each year before such stores would buy and stock their books without going through a (profit-killing) distributor or other middleman?

In the last 15 years, hundreds of independent bookstores have been driven out of business by high rents caused by artificially inflated real estate prices. Did the owners of such stores get any protection from writers, though it was precisely this type of bookstore that kept literature alive?

Most writers older than 45 got their impetus to write because they could accumulate a library out of 95 cent and $1.95 paperbacks. Now, these same books come in $10 to $14 trade paperbacks. Are those established writers going to go to bat in some way so a poor young person can buy their books and bring a new generation of readers into our society?

The National Writers Union reports that each week more and more grievances from writers pile up on its desks. Are all the signers of all the petitions hooting for the survival of NEA going to lend their expertise and the weight of their reputations to aid this organization in defense of writers getting cheated on contracts with publishers?

PEN regularly tries to bail some incarcerated foreign writer named Puck Wow out of difficulty; this is fine, but have you ever heard of them going to the defense of an American writer, even though censorship is more prevalent in this country than almost any other industrialized society? Try to write PEN: They will refer you to the Writers Union, to which only a few of their own members belong.

On the subject of such injustices, I had a brief run-in with Nadine Gordimer nine years ago, ironically at a conference in Mexico City entitled, "The Languages of Colonialism." I heard Nadine say to the packed auditorium, "I want my writing to speak for those who are voiceless." I later asked her how the "voiceless" would ever read her when Penguin was selling her books for the equivalent of $1, U. S., a lot of money across the border. I also asked her why she couldn't ask the sponsors of the event to bus in some interested students from the poor *barrios* of Mexico City if she was so concerned about those voiceless people she claimed to be writing for.

"What you need, young fellow," she said, (damned if I'm young!) "is a writers' cooperative. Something like Writers and Readers."

I always thought it was in the best interests of writers to cooperate, that it was instinctive and natural to cooperate. I feel like Seymour Krim (quoted in *Poets & Writers* by Gerald Nicosia) when he said, "Why can't writers just talk to one another as people? Why do they always shy away from talking about the things that matter in their work? It's foolish to be bitter because your talent is not as big as someone else's."

Krim is right. Writers aren't talking about the things that matter, not in their books, not in their workshops, not in their endless conferences. For the last 25 years what I've observed is competition, a lot in the writers under 50, a little less in the writers over 50.

Precisely because they treat it as a game, they are vulnerable to attack from without, fragile to the point of hysteria, as witnessed by the current debacle of their threatened institution, the NEA. But it was not until it was threatened from without that writers have treated NEA as their institution.

In bits and pieces, reviewers and critics such as Robert Peters, Jonathan Yardley, Lewis Lapham, Hayden Carruth and Richard Kostelanetz have been fussing over the mediocrity in U.S. writing for the last 15 years. But it wasn't till Tom Wolfe rang the church bells of alarm in *Harpers'* magazine in 1990 that writers got upset. Here was a best-selling author attacking them in a national journal. Much like severed ethnic groups in the Balkans, writers could only find unity in what they perceived as the oppressor outside their nationalistic boundaries. As Vanilla Tom went across the U.S. holding town meetings (usually for a handsome fee), writers showed up in vast herds, willing to pay $10 to $20, not to hear him, not to discuss the issues he had raised, but to register in quavering voices their disapproval that he would have the audacity to lump them all under the word "anemic."

1980 was the year of literature's Watergate, some masterful shenanigans in the awarding of individual grants that was generally labeled "cronyism." It was more like theft, and it was investigated by Hilary Masters and finally published (in edited form) in the *George Review* after being rejected by 17 other magazines. Outrage abounded; it was a legitimate public scandal. Yet, heaven help our stale metaphors if we have any public discussion of the so-called "poetry mafia". The arts, especially literature, are a reminder of the purity of our essential beings and must be kept hush-hush lest they be examined like the other breakdowns in our society.

* * *

This form of schizophrenia is no exception. The real master of it is Lewis Lapham, editor of *Harper's*, who has written what I consider to be the best essay on the state of U.S. writing. It's called "The Audible Silence" and was published in a literary quarterly whose identity I couldn't decipher from the Xerox copy Lapham mailed to me. "Given the brilliance of this article," I wrote to him, "and your connections in the media, why didn't you publish this in a more conspicuous journal?"

Lapham wrote back, "My friends told me that if I tried to publish this, I could put my career in a bottle and cast it in the wine-dark sea." With no apologies to Homer, Lapham, like a whole lot of others, is going to have it both ways. From time to time they'll poke at the system, but not so much and not in a way that could jeopardize their comfortable careers. Do not their "careers" summarize the lack of real examination we've had of a country in crisis?

Given an entire nation of careerists, is it any wonder language is now inflated to the point it hardly has any meaning? The repercussions of all this horse shit by these "professionals" are to isolate those writers who could really make a difference, who believe literature is not just a parlor game but the very conscience of a nation.

One such man who's been isolated because he does not play the game is Robert Peters. For 30 years Peters has been producing strong poetry, criticism and drama. But he would offer that most traitorous of ideas: You can never tell where you'll find truly vital writing.

This single idea usurps the whole daisy chain of institutional thinking. It is unforgivably populist. It throws "taste" to the four winds with the money crowd which is the only crowd that can now afford art. Most of all, Peters is unforgivably himself, free of cant and preconceptions; as such, he is an ugly threat to the current epidemic of digested fear and smug cautiousness.

The NEA has acknowledged Peters with a grant but it doesn't make any difference. The NEA literature section long ago fell into the trap of seeing writing as a means and not an end in itself, writers must see the NEA, and any other institution which affects writing, as their rightful home and not a sugar daddy for tough times. In short, for the NEA to have any meaning, there would have to be a revolution in the thinking of the people it benefits. Then, the NEA and its congressional backers would have to come to the understanding that "the first rule for any artist," as Brendan Behan said, "is to be against government."

I doubt that either of the two responsibilities will come to pass. As with a houseful of bedding filled with smallpox, the only way to rid the house of infection is to drag the bedding outside and set it on fire. A lot of sociologists and economists are predicting that social justice will soon come about through some cataclysm they can't name. Writers can't name it either but, like so many of the "experts," they are restless for this change. They may be shocked to discover the change has nothing to do with words, that it is too late for words. In the words of Jean Giono (a writer nobody reads), "People think only of adding to their comfort, heedless that one day true men will come up from the river and down from the mountain, more implacable and more bitter than the grass of the apocalypse."

field notes from a cuban jail: on b. traven

The writer B. Traven went right to the Center of Hell and walked out the other side with a gold crown on his head and a smile on his face. B. Traven is the King of Writers, for this century and for most other centuries. He wrote deftly and quietly with none of the bombast that periodically sneaks into the works of Miller and Bukowski; there is not a hint of the literary mannerism that dominates the so-called classics that are taught in the world's classrooms. He writes from the comparative isolation of villages, mountains, jungles, ships at sea about people who do not have passports, social security cards, or any kind of identifying papers. According to the authorities these people do not exist, have never existed, yet most of our comforts – our teacups and our teabags, our tennis shoes and our stereos – are made by these Faceless of the Earth whose Hell if we bothered to think about it would make us vomit our croissants and decaffeinated coffee. The Twentieth Century is one vast shithole, unremitting and pissing on us by the hour. Traven was there; he sang and fought and danced in its flames. And when we are finished with a Traven book, we look up at the sky and we say, "Thanks, dear Sun God, for allowing me to breathe one more day."

For Traven not only documented the tortures of the damned, he showed us how to persevere with grace, with laughter, with a terrible strength that if we bothered to utilize it, every precinct captain from Fairbanks to Tierra del Fuego would quake in his patent-leather boots and sneak out the backdoor to his sheepfarm. Traven's heroes and heroines suffer every physical deprivation, every grief, every possible insult to their dignity and yet I always feel strong and complete when I finish a Traven book. Like all real writers,

Traven alerts us to the fact that we create our lives, not some boss, not the government, not some company, not some regal institution in Oshkosh, Wisconsin or San Jose, Costa Rica. Us and us alone. In the middle of nowhere. Where civilization as we know it barely reaches.

His heroes and heroines are intensely practical; only in the case of a couple of village school teachers do they have much formal education; though they have been touched by the drift of socialist ideology so prevalent in the first 30 years of this century, they belong to no party and adhere to no ideology. His white heroes, like Traven himself, have strayed far from their origins and are perpetual students of nature, of primitive civilizations, and the effect of civilization on these primitive holdings near the jungle or in the mountains. Though Traven wrote from 1920 to 1968, what he does is recreate the first conflicts between the white man and the Indian; if the white men are alone they tend to respect the world of the mestizo and the Indian; if they are on vacation or represent a company, they view the brown-skin man and woman as primitives who stand in the way of the white man's fortune. In the last seven books that he wrote, Traven increasingly takes on the point of view of the Indians of Southern Mexico, and the real miracle of the man who was B. Traven is born in these books.

For what finally emerges is a rebirth of certain words that have had the sauce wrung from them till they are dry pods. I am thinking of words like dignity, friendship, community, love, eternity, devotion, and freedom. Political sects and organized religions have got a hold of those words and used them as fronts to bully us and cow us and make us sit in the front row with our heads down, ashamed we were born, crying out internally for Jesus or Ronald or Dear Joseph Stalin or Reconstructivism or Mao Tse-Tung or a new compact disc player to take our dreary souls and toss them away and outfit us with a new allegiance so that we are not so lonely, so that we might feel we after all belong somewhere. A Traven hero is very happy to be alive; life begins there, it begins with an allegiance to the dawn, a song, a personal prayer, a poem the way all Indians used to do when they stood at the door of their hut or teepee which always faced East. In other words life must begin each day with a sense of humility. It must begin with the notion that human beings – if that word is to have any meaning – are a part of a large and amazing creation, of which man is surely not the centerpiece. This was the foundation of the Traven philosophy and it flies in the face of everything we have been taught.

Traven was a moralizer and a teacher, generally two occupations which will put us to sleep in a hurry. But he wove his vision with such patience in a framework of leisurely storytelling with such attentiveness to detail and tone that we follow him with complete trust. There is that thing in Traven that no amount of rational thinking or literary criticism can account for: that is the sixth sense that every sentiment, every detail has been earned. And this happens because I don't think Traven was ever worried about being a writer; he no doubt had concerns that his writing would pull in enough to feed him but I'm sure he felt he would survive somehow, some way.

No, I think what really concerned Traven was the question that no one I meet wants to talk about, that no one I meet wants to think about, that few writers or artists ever consider in their creations: how to be a man (or a woman) without being a bully? Or put another way, can we gain our food and lodging and sense of self-importance without enslaving others? Every ounce of Traven is addressed to this question at all times. And what if 99% of the people we meet or are going to meet in our lifetime have been so used to one form or another of slavery that it makes it impossible to treat them as free and equal persons? How to break this vicious chain of coerce or be coerced? It is this that turns us into dead men long before we are dead, that keeps us from enjoying life in our brief time on this earth. Each upheaval, each revolution, each turn in social, cultural, or political fashion has only put a new bully on the block, and each time people's subservience has become more pronounced. One hundred and ten years ago, a brilliant thinker in the fertile and lugubrious Russian mold named Vissarion Belinsky wrote, "What good does freedom do me if my neighbor is in chains?" "In each person there is a free soul and a slave and they fight for domination," wrote Maxim Gorky 30 years later.

Céline wasn't so generous. On this planet, he wrote, "one can lie or die." Céline wrote this in 1935 from Paris after prolonged visits to Africa and the United States. Traven, on the other hand, had the luck of a unique time and a highly original place. He arrived from Germany via China in Tampico, Mexico, in 1924; more important, within two years he would find himself in Chiapas, Mexico, one of the most unique areas in the world then and now. For it was only four years ago, 1992, that Chiapas exploded across the world's newspapers and magazines because of a rebellion among various offshoots of the Tsotsil Indians – the very Indians that Traven wrote about – that expanded into an expression of many Mexicans the desire for a new ruling party. The implications reached far beyond Mexico and the Mexican stock market in which U.S., Canadian, and European investors have pumped more than a billion dollars during the past 15 years. At stake was the whole Indian slave system of Latin America where a tiny elite govern much the way they did 80 years ago. The Mexican stock market could not be allowed to collapse; not when Mexican workers would assemble televisions and stereo systems for eight or ten dollars a day and lordly investors could smile from their armchairs in Frankfurt, Tokyo, and New York at the lordly dividends rolling in. Thus, President Clinton could commit millions of dollars to keep the Mexican Bolsa from collapsing. The teacups and electric dildos of the investors' mistresses were at stake.

As men from the world's financial institutions met at mahogany tables to see what could be done, CNN was interviewing students in Chiapas. These students were holding aloft two books, Eduardo Galeano's *Open Veins of Latin America* and B. Traven's *Rebellion of the Hanged*. You would have thought such exposure would send a few book buyers to the store to check out Traven. But no such thing happened; the audience of intelligent people for an unusual author remained and remains hopelessly comfortable, hopelessly bored, hopelessly passive. I am writing this from a country in Latin America which attracts several thousand tourists each week from all the developed countries. For the last month I've been asking these tourists – many of them quite well-read – if the name B. Traven means anything to them? With all of them I get a shake of the head until I mention *The Treasure of the Sierra Madre* and then I get a smile of recognition.

At any rate, Chiapas had come full circle since the time of Traven. What he discovered there in 1924 was that the Mexican Revolution had just terminated. All of Mexico buzzed with a new belief in justice; workers organized; schools were built; the church was relegated to the back burner in the reorganization of this new society. This was also the period when the U.S. corporations and the U.S. government had its nose in every banana republic and was installing dictators who would make sure the fruit cocktail on American tables was picked by illiterates who were compensated with just enough money to survive. In Mexico, the U.S. oil companies were traipsing through every Eastern pueblo looking for gold, looking for oil, looking for anything cheap to buy so they could sell it for 500% profit in good old Oshkosh. Traven wrote about this in *The White Rose*, how an Indian chief is abducted by a U.S. oil company to get his land. But books have no power; they are nothing, paper to light the trash in the family incinerator. But a movie, a movie, ahh now we are talking. So when the Mexican film version of this book won all of the major Latin American awards in 1963, the U.S. State Department banned it from entering the United States. They did not think it important enough to ban Traven because no one was reading him anyway. It was around this year that Traven returned much of the advance monies to Alfred Knopf because a particular book did not sell even 3,000 copies.

But history has an odd way of coming back to piss on our dreams and our credit cards. In 1935, President Lázaro Cárdenas nationalized many of the oil holdings and tossed out the American drillers. It was his son who in 1986 launched a series of candidacies around the platform of the completion of the 1910 Revolution that stirred the Lacandons and the Chamulas – Traven's old friends – who in turn began to rumble and made the bolsas tremble from Mexico City to Wall Street. History keeps coming at us and coming at us. Because what I am really talking about here – hoping somehow to reach you between your second croissant and your addiction to the *New York Times* – is nature. It is nature's nature not only to murder us in our sleep but to give and give and give, to shower us with all the delights of its startling womb – tasty fish, magnificent sunsets, shade to cool us, sun to heal our chests. It is in our nature – because we are nature too – to give but how many people do we know who can give, who have anything to give? People cannot give for the simple reason that they don't know how to take, take what nature has provided for them. They take the wrong things. When they don't get them, they start to push other people. They make ideas; they think these ideas will control people and make something they call "society" better. They build a building to put the ideas in. Then they hire the least intelligent but the most aggressive of their kind to guard the building lest anyone try to break in and steal the idea. It is all crazy. But then we are crazy – me, you, almost everything that we have built. We are not men, we are not women. We are things, even less animated than the furniture we buy; we are moved here, moved there. We think ourselves free, but on only a few occasions in my 50 years have I met a free man.

I met one the other day. I happened to be passing time in a Cuban jail. It seems I had slugged what I thought was a hotel worker who'd advised me the woman by my side was a prostitute and could not enter the hotel bar. Now let it be known that I am a great defender of women's rights. I will defend to my dying breath the right of any woman to sit on my head for $10.00 an hour. To all of my seven ex-wives I paid four times that and the law had advised us we could "do it" legally. Well, it turned out that the hotel worker was really an undercover cop; I should have known because he spoke English with a Boston accent. They said I had broken his nose and that it would be weeks before his wife or his mistress would kiss him; I had disfigured him so badly.

The cops had their doubts; I am grey-haired and spindly and fifty; I don't look like a match for a strong wind. The Cuban cops kept going back to the room where the hotel worker-cop was being interviewed so they could peek under his bandages to ascertain that I had really done the damage I was purported to have done. They saw the stitches and the misshapen nose that no girl in her right mind would kiss and they returned to harangue me with "Capitalist Pig."

I fully admit to being a capitalist pig; that is why this essay took so long to get written to complete a book that nobody in their right mind would want to read. Why should I work for four weeks, ten hours a day at a project that will never earn me a carton of Marlboro Lights when I can travel to the Cuban countryside, buy a 1953 or '54 Topps Mickey Mantle baseball card for $48.00, fly to New York and sell it for several thousand dollars, return to Havana where I can hire three beautiful women for ten dollars an hour to take turns sitting on my face and singing the revolutionary songs from the Sierra Maestra days when a man was a man and sugar grew outside every palapa. You tell me. For these girls all have an uncle who took potshots at Meyer Lansky coming out of the Havana Hilton with a mulatta hooker on each arm and a bottle of Cutty Sark in his white tuxedo jacket. And when the girls get done biting my tonsils and mopping my floors, they sing the song, indeed the anthem of the old banana companies of United Fruit, "Yes, We Have No Bananas." We are all happy and the world of culture is not any worse for me not having written an overdue essay.

But what got me thinking about Traven and my debt to him was a very shabby man who gave me a pack of cigarettes while I was contemplating my navel in a Cuban jail. He was visiting a cousin who'd been arrested for selling black market onions and he happened to notice the Mormon Tabernacle Choir of Cops singing, "Capitalist Pig." He handed me a pack of cigarettes, which by the way cost him the equivalent of two days' wages, and said, "You need these worse than I do." This more than the police took the starch right out of me. All my pugilism melted and I thought, "Traven writes about just such people; perhaps it's my duty to talk about them." So the authorities were gracious enough to let me read Traven, largely because they could not locate my passport. I'd handed my bag with my passport to the insulted girl and she'd fled. Prostitution in Cuba has a sentence of four years in prison.

So, while a hundred policemen searched for the girl, another six policemen (Cuban intelligence) were plowing through every file, every computer printout for the identity of "William Stubbs," "Renaldo Hemingway," and finally, "William Joyce." Friends kept bringing the copies of Traven's books I had stored in my apartment so I was actually enjoying my new home, though the food was lousy and I sometimes had to read with the aid of a Zippo lighter. The only "William Joyce" who turned up on the computer weighed 225 pounds, was six-foot three inches, and was said to be promoting evangelical Baptist religion. I weigh 170 pounds, am 5 foot 11 inches and do not know the words to "Go Tell It on the Mountain."

Quirk of quirks, coincidence of coincidences. The same thing that made me reread Traven was the exact cause for him writing in the first place – loss of any identifying papers.

Traven carried no papers because Germany put a death sentence on his head for treason. After World War I, Traven belonged to a group that wanted to organize a socialist state in a separatist Bavaria. Traven's closest associates were caught and executed. Traven got away; after hiding in various European countries, harassed and deported because he had no papers, he caught a ship from Antwerp to China, and from China he caught another ship for Mexico where he landed under an alias in 1924.

In his first novel *Death Ship*, in a passage that he later deleted from the book, Traven launches its principal theme that would later prepare him mentally to discover the world of the Indian. "The weaklings have always good police records and fine passports. And it is the weaklings and the cowards that make the criminals of the big cities. A strong heart knows how to struggle and he likes to struggle for his life." Traven lied about who he was and where he had been. The reading public, he said, was not entitled to a man's history nor his personality, only to his work. It was this denial and evasiveness about his background that ironically excited the reading public and the press. To date there have been more than 40 books and 500 articles about "the real B. Traven" but not a single book about the value of his writing. In 1948, after the release of John Huston's *The Treasure of the Sierra Madre*, there were more than 300 European, American, and Mexican journalists running around Mexico looking for Traven, who had disguised himself as an innkeeper in Acapulco, Mexico. By this time, his books had been translated into 23 languages (from the original German, even though Traven usually tried to pass himself off as an American, writing in a butchered English slang) and had sold millions of copies. But in the U.S.A., a few thousand; and perhaps it is this mystery which should be talked about, not the abiding mystery of "*THE REAL B. TRAVEN.*" Shirley Cloyes, director of the former publisher of Traven, Frederick Hill, says the poor sales are because of Traven's aversion to publicity. Fine, but does that explain his phenomenal sales in Europe where he had an almost equal lack of publicity? A separate book needs to be written on why U.S. reading audiences are so different from

European and Latin American and Japanese readers. Then we would have some understanding why our grand republic remains so alone, so dominant and so isolated in world affairs. Part of the answer is that historically, other original writers have suffered the same neglect as Traven. I am thinking of Cossery (Egypt), Giono (France), Voinovich (Russia), Kohout and Hrabal (Czechoslovakia), Jules Renard (France), Elias Canetti (Bulgaria and Germany), Donoso (Chile), Carpentier (Cuba). These are huge, original talents that take your breath away and make you go back to them again and again. It's true that the American character is generous, especially toward underdogs; that is in our psyche and our history. But what that same character does with artists of any originality is abominable. It relishes inventors but cannot stand thinkers; like its step-sister England, it worships cleverness at the expense of any real profundity. Its geographical remoteness and horrid education system have made it disdain cultures different from itself. The United States is not alone in trying to exterminate its Indians, but it is alone in trying to cut their hair and shove an alien culture clown their throats. For two centuries now we have thought we were the best, and at many things we were; but in the end we have proved ourselves the most divisive and the most lonely. An American alone in a foreign capital is always a bit more lonely than a German or a Dane or an Argentinian. We have separated ourselves from the rest of the nations and we will pay a terrible price for it.

For example, in a famous short story called "Assembly Line" Traven dramatizes the relationship between Indian values and U.S. commercial rapaciousness; at the same time, he once and for all defines the relationship between the artist and an entire world ignorant of what goes into his art but desires it nevertheless.

The Indian weaves baskets in amazing symphonies of color and design that reflect his love and interpretation of the natural world. Says Traven, "the most amazing thing was that these decorations were not painted on the baskets but were instead actually part of the baskets themselves. Bast and fibers dyed in dozens of different colors were so cleverly – one must actually say intrinsically – interwoven that those attractive designs appeared on the inner part of the basket as well as on the outside." Though each basket has woven in it, birds and antelopes, tigers and squirrels, and may take 40 to 60 hours to produce, the Indian artist made only the equivalent of pennies and was treated shabbily as he went door to door in this Mexican town selling his wares. Traven puts it all in perspective when he says, "He (the Indian) had little knowledge of the outside world or he would have known that what happened to him was happening every hour of every day to every artist all over the world. That knowledge would perhaps have made him very proud, because he would have realized he belonged to the little army which is the salt of the earth and which keeps culture, urbanity, and beauty for their own sake from passing away." Perhaps Traven is being ironic about culture and urbanity. At any rate, the Indian gets a visitor – Mr. E.L. Winthrop, fresh from a Rotarian convention in Hot Springs, Arkansas. E.L. goes gaga over the sight of the little baskets; right away he sees them as an explosive bestseller on the New York market with an Easter egg in every basket and chicks hatching all over the continent. Pregnant to the point of hysteria with his marketing idea, Winthrop flies to New York where he convinces a candy merchant to buy ten thousand baskets. Traven's description of the psychology of the candy merchant defines once and for all the mentality of the modem entrepreneur: "Never before had he seen anything like them (the baskets) for originality, prettiness, and good taste. He, however, avoided most carefully *showing any sign of enthusiasm* (italics mine), for which there would be time enough once he knew the price and whether he could get a whole load exclusively."

Here in a few words, Traven dissects a whole civilization. The confectioner is no barbarian; he fully recognizes quality when he sees it. But he's instinctively ready to pare his emotions; emotions are not good for business. Damned if he is going to display any enthusiasm; that might make him lose leverage. Leverage, my friends, is what modern society is all about. We can't show people how we feel because we might end up on the short end.

Eventually, feeling itself atrophies; we become ghosts, pushed this way and that, whichever way the market dictates. The beauty, intelligence, joy, wholeness we were born with is subdivided into lots, all for sale under conditions which have more to do with asphalt and little to do with clear eyes and a smile that reflects the power of the sun. In such a subdivided face, the teeth take over, not with the enthusiasm of eating and relishing the nourishment provided by the earth and man's adaptive intelligence, but teeth that masticate, teeth that slash and grind at the fiber of soul and do so out of a sense of impotency to fill the vacuum in the subdivided face that can no longer see, no longer hear, no longer sing. Emotion is the binder for body, mind, and spirit. When it is pared away in the name of marketing, the face caves in on itself, the liver and spleen crackle like dry tinder. Soon, atomic fusion. Power for sure, but no creation; particles of molecules subdivided like the earth itself for underground parking lots. The soul of man ready to buckle under to the next bully on the block for it can no longer resist. Subdivided, no body can heal, and without healing there can be no love. Not romantic love but the love as reflected in Traven's book, *The Bridge in the Jungle*, where the white, civilized narrator can say at the end of a funeral to bury a young Indian boy, "He is my boy, my little brother, my fellow man who could suffer as I can, who could laugh as I can, and who could die as I shall die some day."

There was not merely a gap between what we know as white civilization and Indian culture, there was a positive wall which can never be climbed unless the so-called educated Western man relinquishes his statuary Ego and walks into the Indian village naked and on Indian terms. For in 1926, as a guide for German archeological teams, Traven entered such villages of the Chamulas and the Lacandons. Everything in his life had prepared him for their world. He wanted desperately to find a place and a people where the word community meant something. He found it and it is reflected in *Bridge* which is the centerpiece of his writing. In this book there come together all the themes mentioned in the earlier books: the greed of individuals, but more often the corporations and oil companies to the north of Mexico; the ingeniousness, playfulness and capacity for sorrow of these Mayan Indians; the words freedom and dignity and how they work together.

I would like to say a word about the latter and then leave Traven to rest. He is no James Joyce; he is simple and accessible. Go read him, my explanations are not important compared with his patient and wise art.

My last story is a little run-in I had with Traven's Indians and how experience taught me what Traven's books could not. It was 1985 and I was sitting as professor of a writing class of unusually perceptive and hungry students at John Jay College in New York City. And I was not getting through. I was sitting there reading to them from *The Bridge in the Jungle* and alternately trying to explain the phrase, "Con su permiso," and how it captured a way of life different from the one I and my students had been educated in. I wasn't doing a very good job; there are times words fail us when we most need them, when we most want to describe what is important to us.

"With your permission." It seems so polite, so innocuous, but for the next six weeks I was haunted by the phrase. I woke in the middle of the night thinking about it but my head got no clearer in trying to phrase what it meant. Then one morning my fifth wife got a call to be a movie star. She was to be in a film and the film was to be made in Mexico. I was invited to go along. I was still 500 miles from the home of Traven's injuns but I took a bus there and as I was climbing the steps to my hotel, a very young Indian boy bolted out of the doorway and started downward carrying a bicycle twice as big as he was. I should have been the one to stop and let him pass but he reacted much quicker than I did. He dropped the bike, jumped to the side, and said, "Con su permiso." He was maybe 11 years old. Though my Spanish was poor, from reading Traven I knew to say, "Pase." He nodded with a bright smile and left me wiser than I'd been in a long time.

There is more at stake here than a phrase that indicates courtesy or Indian humility. Traven says about this phrase, "To them (the Indians) it was impossible to cut through the breath of a human without having his permission to do so." The space immediately around us is special, inviolable, private. This is not what we own; ownership means nothing; it is what we are that counts. What we are is unequivocally given its space and its privacy. We can stand – according to the Chamula – in Timboctu in rags or on Fifth Avenue in New York in a linen suit and no one can cross our immediate space without asking in a gentle voice, "Con su permiso." In fancier terms, first decreed by the French Revolution, it is called "the rights of the individual."

It also signals me that the Indian in southern Mexico knows we must live by laws higher than the individual as long as those laws do not jeopardize the worth of the individual. And that basic to our every breath is a sense of humility. This does not translate to abjectness as it might in Christian theology. It is the awareness as that awareness connects with every fiber of our being that we as humans are part of a much bigger scheme that includes all things animate, and the worm and the mosquito must be given their due.

It is not the individual versus community, as we are often taught in an eighth-grade civics class, but the individual who instinctively identifies with the needs of the community, especially during crisis periods. When an Indian mother's young son falls from a bridge – constructed without railings by the local American company drilling for oil – and drowns in the river, everyone, even the white narrator, participates in her grief: "Many of the women brought armfuls of flowers; others brought wreaths hastily made out of twigs and covered with

121

gold and silver paper. They put the flowers and the wreaths aside so as to spare the Garcia woman the pain of thanking them." Thus this prolonged death scene in *The Bridge in the Jungle* becomes a great hymn for life as a group of poor people reach out for one another and lift the sorrow of the grieving mother into a candle light that hovers above the entire story. Traven concludes, "It seemed that an occasion such as the one I had witnessed was necessary if one wanted to see those people as they really were, to see not only the dirt and their rags, but, what was more, their hearts and souls, the only things in man which count. Radios, Fords, and speed records do not count at all; they are but garbage when it comes to the final balance sheet."

That word "human" has been blasted to a numbing cliché, but I can think of no other book which so beautifully and resonantly returns that word to its rightful place. I give the final word to Traven: "A trip to a Central American jungle to watch how Indians behave near a bridge won't make you see either the jungle or the bridge or the Indians if you believe that the civilization you were born into is the only one that counts. Go and look around with the idea that everything you learned in school and college is wrong."

the curse of brussels sprouts: richard yates revisited

If you want to know what's wrong with the world, I'll tell you. Blame it all on Brussels sprouts. Blame the wars, the domestic hysteria, the barking dogs, the bawling kids, the corrupt nursing homes, the insane school rooms, the blighted killers who go into school rooms, blame all these things on Brussels sprouts. In addition Brussels sprouts are responsible for that maddening moustache on your mother-in-law's lip.

Whoever invented Brussels sprouts ought to be locked up in a zoo, in the orangutan's cage. Carrots remind me of Bugs Bunny's teeth, broccoli of the brain stem, but Brussels sprouts are just sort of there, little pods with the taste of old cardboard, the odor of institutional walls. They cripple the revival spirit in one of Richard Yates' characters, a guy named Walter Henderson.

Walter's just been sacked from his job and has to tell his wife about it. But on the way home he's had some exciting memories and he's hatched a plan, a devious little scheme to keep his wifey wife in the dark. He's not going to tell her; he's going to pretend to go to work and see what develops from there. Maybe, he'll get another job, maybe he'll marry a pygmy and move to Botswana. The unknownness of his scheme is the fun of it.

But when he opens the door of his apartment, "the first thing that hit him was the smell of Brussels sprouts."

The story, "A Glutton for Punishment," goes on for another 1,500 words but those sprouts signal the end of it. The end of Walter Henderson's resolve to get a little inventiveness, a little intrigue, a little mystery into his life. The fact that he has been fired from a job is irrelevant; he never went to the job anyway. Oh, he was there and the job was there but everybody is just going through the motions of work for a product whose ends they do not know even as they have no idea what they should really be doing in their brief time on this earth. It's a vacuum for sure, one which everyone tries to fill with Brussels sprouts. Tasteless, a grim reminder of the solemn duty of every good citizen, Brussels sprouts cut the legs, the manhood, and the humanhood from under Walter Henderson. If the food is tasteless, the streets tasteless, the offices tasteless, the wife gone dry, the children nagging, there is only one thing to do: buckle up and practice deportment. Walter's first act after the meltdown from the kitchen is to "put his hat *carefully* (italics mine) in the hall closet . . ."

He doesn't want to disturb the prevailing order here at home, or anywhere. Oddly, he would have shaken the order of things, if only for himself, had he been able to go through with his plan to keep his firing a secret. He would have wandered Manhattan's streets, been able to reflect, had odd conversations with people he wouldn't ordinarily speak to, gotten to know Manhattan. Above all, he would have to figure out what to do with his time according to his own fragile sense of pleasure. He might even have started to inch up on a status rarely honored on the planet and least of all in the United States: a man who'd found a way to feel at home on earth.

Yates offers his floundering soul a reprieve just after the attack of the Brussels sprouts: "The children were still at their supper in the kitchen; . . ." Most children I've every encountered are open to anything as long as it doesn't bend them or break them. They would be entirely open to his throwing the Brussels sprouts in the garbage and announcing, "I have a new recipe for hamburgers and I'm going to make it for you but on one condition – mother and dear children have to sing, 'Old MacDonald Had a Farm.'" I think the kids of Henderson would have liked that. The beleaguered, fatigued wife would have gotten back a little energy. And Walter Henderson might have lessened the tension he was carrying and renewed the resolve for hiding-go-seek plans.

But the poor man doesn't even see his children, not at first. What he sees are "the milk cartons, the mayonnaise jars and soup cans and cereal boxes, the peaches lined up to ripen on the windowsill." The familiar and the dull that weigh him down each day. Only then does he see children.

He doesn't greet his kids. Hell no. Instead he goes to the bathroom for more of that fucking deportment. He scrubs himself for about two years. It's "the job of washing up for dinner."

If I've sounded derogatory toward a fictional character, I also have to say I've been there, and continue to be there on rare occasions, suffering the Brussels sprouts till I can collect a few bucks and make my getaway – usually to Borneo or even farther from civilization. As has Yates. He knows we have all been to the same places, carried out the same elaborate charade, sometimes out of pure habit, or to get a paycheck or get laid. We had to serve up Brussels sprouts – a lot of mindnumbing clichés – to fit in wherever we went and now in his written work, Yates is going to serve up our heads on a platter.

It seems so quiet the way he serves up the daily fare from our daily lives. We may be a bit misguided, we think to ourselves, but surely it can't be that bad. By the time we finish two or three Yates stories, or half of a novel, we know it is that bad. In our total acceptance of mere efficiency, the belief in the glory of our machines, the dismal mediocrity that discourages dreams, we have relegated life itself to the back burner till the flame goes out. Then to justify our lives have to look for someone to beat on.

Could it be any other way?

"Sure it could," says Yates. At least in his work I find bits and pieces that suggest that people aren't totally trapped. Yates himself, in an interview, said something different: "If my work has a theme, I suspect it is a simple one: that most human beings are inescapably alone, and therein lies their tragedy."

All of the commentary on Yates in the past ten years reenforces this comment of his about people being cornered with no way out. "Tragically honest", "Brutally honest" ring the refrains. "Rebirth of a dark genius" chimes in another cheerleader, this one 3,000 miles away in London. On and on, in reviews of his reissued books, blogs on the internet, jacket blurbs for the books. Why bother? The author's been dead for 17 years. His books have been out of print for 40 years. And when they were in print they never sold very well.

What is all the fuss about? And has anybody gotten anything right about Yates the second go around? I ask these questions because they sure made a mess of Yates the first time around. Yates did a lot of cooperating with them but not in his work. And finally the work is all we have, the only real testament we have on what we may have missed in not paying more attention to Richard Yates.

When I say "they" I have a very specific crowd in mind. But perhaps I should say "we"; I was there when the books were going out of print. I was at the famous Iowa Writers' Workshop when Yates was popping Benzedrine pills by the water fountain so he'd have enough steam to go back inside our classroom and conduct a class called, "American Literature 406". Looking back 42 years, I can say that Yates cut out any facile generalizing by making students go right to the text to back up any assertions they made. I liked that. And I liked the way he really listened when students spoke. He responded, too, in a way that he had no prior agenda, the way teachers usually do, but only a desire to follow the evidence that was in front of him and move from there to some logical conclusion. It seems simple enough but I've been around classrooms enough to know there are very few teachers, or writer/teachers, who ever do it. It takes energy, patience, and a willingness to involve yourself with something that may not confer any personal benefit.

What I didn't like about Yates was the extraordinary strain

he put on himself to run a class. He held himself very rigid and periodically this managing a class turned into a performance but I couldn't say what kind, a strain coming from somewhere else and known only to Yates.

Perhaps it was his sense of being dismissed as a writer. In the fall of 1967, when I took a hardback copy of *Eleven Kinds of Loneliness* to his literature class to have him autograph it, he barked, "Right off the remainder stack, huh?"' I'd bought the book for 99 cents and it was a week later after I'd read the stories that I felt stunned that such a book could be sold for 99 cents and that such an author would have to teach to pay his monthly rent.

I knew then something was badly wrong – with everything – but in 1967 I couldn't have articulated what was wrong. I was ignorant about most everything. It wasn't that I'd been sheltered, quite the opposite. Nor had I spent much time around books and I certainly, even then, didn't take institutions very seriously. I had buoyancy but it wasn't anything I felt I could show in public unless it was an occasional game of touch football or softball.

I mention my buoyancy because I recall Yates saying once to a small group of us students that someone he'd known had written him that his stories had left the guy depressed for three days. The remark stands out in my memory because it was the opposite of what I felt about *Eleven Kinds of Loneliness*.

My reaction was pure silence; I sat at the desk in my windowless one-room apartment very still. I didn't feel the need to do anything or think anything. I felt more self-contained than I could ever remember feeling. I was at peace and I was grateful. After perhaps five minutes like this, I said to myself, "Well, somebody's finally said it." That was my total reaction. I felt lighter than before and I felt no need to analyze what I'd just read.

I would be at Iowa another ten months; during that period I read all sorts of authors – some were required reading for courses, others I read because students said they were in vogue. Always during that time I came back to Yates. Maybe just a few paragraphs, sometimes an entire story. This would happen maybe once every two months. There was a strength there, of a non-literary sort; hanging on to a few paragraphs of Yates I found a solidity I didn't know anywhere else. Thanks to him I felt grounded but not in any way that hemmed me in.

Yates had nothing to do with teaching me how to write. I've never been worried about learning how to write because, then and now, when I sit before a typewriter I feel calm, as if everything is going to take care of itself. It was life, and more particularly being around people, that I struggled with. I didn't so much read as I clawed at the pages hoping they'd give me some hint of how I should conduct myself. Somebody who could give me clarity about what was going on out there. As soon as you want something from somebody all the shit starts. Yates advised me (now I can articulate it) not to want too much from other people and in the care in which he relayed this message, I knew I should occasionally ask a lot from myself. The latter was the only thing that made life fun. People were innately builders; go find something to build.

That was then.

But there is something else in Yates that I, and everyone else, should have paid more attention to – the river. The river is the opposite of Brussels sprouts; it's the opposite even when it's a stinky river, a yellow sulphuric river, because a river is always flowing; it comes from an important source – the mountains – and it is headed toward its glorious end – the sea. Walter Henderson and his wife, before she was wifey wife, go there (at girlfriend's instigation). Yates relays this as part of Walter's reverie as he retraces the steps to this romance after he's been fired. "I love the river at this time of day," she had told him. But on revisiting the scene of his romantic triumph his vision is this, "he was standing at the little balustrade, looking down at the swarm of sleek cars on the East River Drive and at the slow, gray water moving beyond it." That's it, that's all. Already the bud of that blossoming romance that led to marital coupling has dried up. The river has flattened out for Walter Henderson and it's not that Walter Henderson's name is common or Yates' characters so ordinary but that they make themselves common – flattened out – because of how they interpret the guiding glows that are offered to them. When Walter first starts toward the river to review that magical evening, he sees it in these terms: "Starting down alone, he found it strengthening to have one clear triumph to look back on – one time in his life, at least, when he had denied the possibility of failure, and won." The world of Yates is so exacting, so precise, note the little comma just after "failure"; Yates wants a hesitation and then an announcement of "AND WON."

Like most of us, and certainly those budding writers gathered around Yates in Iowa in 1967, Walter sees the river as a prop for a conquest. Not only is all of life measurable for him, it is easily definable in terms of Won and Lost. Winners and Losers, Losers and Winners. We, as readers, have no idea what Walter and his future wife said to each other, what little bits of companionship crept in among the grass and the flow of the river. We just know that Walter has triumphed because, "he had drawn her close and kissed her for the first time." In other words, the guy's been waiting all evening, perhaps his entire life, for just this measurable proof that he's not a failure.

No wonder then for us, or for Yates, a preposterous burden is conferred on each potential romance. It's not movement that counts but accountability – winning. That's why Walter, like so many of Yates' characters, carries such a load of self-consciousness. They are always watching themselves to see how they're doing. Simultaneously, they are actors, script writers, directors and producers. There is no spontaneity, except in failure: "They got me," Walter announces to his wife at the end of the story.

Neither can there be personality in a Richard Yates story. Personalities rarely exist in U.S. writing. What we get in Yates are levels of degradation, sometimes little more than flailing nerve endings, people down to their last resources of bone marrow and a scream as in the salesman in the novel *Disturbing the Peace*. True, Yates does create an admirable drill sergeant but he's definable within the limits of his job, and when he's transferred from his passion, from his level of competence, there is no one to defend him. To have personality you have to have elbow space and you have to have time. Yates' characters are almost defined by their busyness; physically, they are always crowded by people and things. Rarely do you see clouds, trees, the sky. It's a people-dominated world and dominated too by the things people make: milk cartons, mayonnaise jars, etc., etc. People cram anything and everything into this vacuum where neither clouds nor personalities can reach and it is all pretty much like the world we know: hysteria threatening at each turn of a Yates' sentence even as his characters straighten one last misplaced forelock, pull the necktie a little tighter, turn the noose of deportment one last notch before the Grim Reaper chops their nuts off and they sing contralto in the sky with a quartet of archangels. For to have personality, to enjoy life . . . just a little, you have to forget measurement, certainly where your own efforts are concerned, and spend a little more time alongside the river where you don't try to prove anything, just shut off the mind and enjoy the flow, or if you have to talk, tell a good joke, put out some squirrel feed, do anything as long as it's inconsequential.

What I'm talking about here, and I think Yates was talking about, is somehow lessening the load we bear. Yates' fictional characters always feel to me like they are bent in the back, stooped; they carry too heavy a load. Gravity threatens to bury each Yates' paragraph in a heap of sludge and what rescues it is Yates' own spectacular calmness at the center of his debacle. He is calm because he is slowly burrowing his way out the morass we call "civilization" or maybe just "making it", or "getting ahead." He may have had this large reputation for being ragged and being a mess but I'm convinced he was never a mess at the typewriter. He may be the most circumspect writer who's ever put a scalpel to society.

But the rage is there. I felt it at age 25, and I see it clearly now in the very careful orchestration of his words and his paragraphs. It's the rage of a man who feels he's been fed nothing but lies and is going to mirror them back at the perpetrators and make them retreat into a corner with no escape. This is revenge-minded writing and there is no cornering it under the euphemisms of "realism" or "neo-naturalism" that are often bandied about in the better periodicals. Neither does it help to say that Yates was a "literary genius" or "rebel." At 25 when I was first reading Yates, I'd just finished Heller's *Catch-22* and Céline's *Journey to the End of the Night*. Now there are a pair of literary geniuses, at least to the halfway point of Heller when inventiveness gives out and you notice all the bare ribs of his literary machinery. Or Céline who can never resist make the hind-end of his sentences rear back like a scorpion's tail to sting the pus-ridden constructions of mankind one last time. With those two brilliant souls you know you are dealing with just books. Literary ones, but still books. Yates' uniqueness was the elaborate pains he took to conceal literary artifice, probably because he knew books ultimately were just as suspect as everything else, including Brussels sprouts.

Should Yates have done more?

I think we make a mistake with our writers in the same way we ask too much of our husbands, wives, drill instructors whose systems cannot protect them. The very fine Czech writer, Bohumil Hrabal, once told me, "I am just a link in a chain," and he rattled off some 15 writers he said were in large part responsible for the arrival of his books. Each writer can only do a little bit; in some clumsy way, Yates led me to Hrabal and Hrabal led me to Kohout and Kohout led me to Elias Canetti which led me to a dark corner one morning where I sang, "Old MacDonald Had a Farm," eee-aiii, eeyi, yo. There is no upward ascendancy with writers or anything else. We are all born very beautiful and half-way smart; we are all born lovers and warriors and if we think otherwise, it's because we've allowed others to convince us we are dull and mediocre and ought to have Brussels sprouts every night for dinner. It's what Yates was saying: from the beginning someone is always trying to lay their agenda on us to reduce us to their level of mediocrity. And everyone falls for it.

What I've just said usurps the whole notion of a pantheon of literary giants up there in the sky whom we ought to pay attention to. Reviewers and critics are now trying to put Yates in some golden triangle with Hemingway and Fitzgerald, or Hemingway and Faulkner, or Faulkner and the Dalai Lama. All those guys were just like you and me: dreary fuckups who drank too much and occasionally fell off the barstool. And their work shows it. If they had the good fortune and talent and perseverance to write 15 or 20 illuminating short stories or one or two terrific novels, that doesn't make them god-heads, not in literature, or even at the local bar. There is no magic throne and there are no experts, just 80 or 100 writers who entertained me and inched me along toward some self-realization, a snotty little waif less gravity-bound.

Neither do I believe there are a lot of good books out there and you got your pick. There is a hierarchy of writers floating out there but for me it is always changing: 20 years ago I would have sworn Alejo Carpentier and a Colombian named Arcinieagas were right at the top; today I'll take my stance with Nikolai Gogol and Jean Giono. But whoever I lean toward I have to thank Richard Yates for freeing me up (and he wasn't the only one) to feel free and make choices independent of what anyone else thought. It wasn't so much what he introduced me to at a tender age as what he made me recognize from where I'd been and all the silly compromises I'd made. Words, he said, in some odd way were a matter of conscience and not ever something for the market or to appease a human being.

Yes, I might have asked for some levity and a little more companionship from Yates, but that would have been asking too much. I would find those qualities in other writers, or sometimes writers not at all but squirrels, birds, stray cats, and the hum of crickets at night. My mistake was in thinking that because I'd stepped a little away from Yates that I'd gone beyond him. When you do that as I did, you've not only mis-calculated your reach but that you are now subject to just how ruthless and bitter the entire race is, especially in the U.S. of A.

As to why Yates isn't thought more highly of, better to ask the question why humans are so far from each other. And why it has been this way for a long time. First, of the 60 to 80 writers that have lit the way for me, only a handful are still in print. This raises the further questioning of just what is publishing. Surely it's more than just getting a manuscript between a binding and putting it on some bookshelf for seven weeks or four months. Okay, there's that paperback edition so the writer has another eight months or perhaps even two years of life before the potential reader.

But shouldn't publishing be more than that? Among all those offices in New York, Boston, and San Francisco aren't there bright, adventurous souls who are going to establish some sort of priorities and maintain before our eyes the best our tribe has created? It's naive of me to think so, and would have been naive in 1920. Unless it's been the old Grove Press or James Laughlin's New Directions, there's never been a genuine publisher in the United States. The brightness or adventurousness in those young editors' eyes soon gets swal-lowed up delivering Brussels sprouts, the companionship of rivers drowned in the conventional wisdom that publishing is a business too, and the success of life is in who wins and who loses and who ascends to a special dais and gets labeled STAR.

At The Writers' Workshop, I got a lesson in this too, just 20 or 30 yards from where I first met Richard Yates. In this instance the instructor was John Irving, not John Irving the famous writer, but John Irving the teaching assistant, like I was, and he was teaching me how to organize a grade book.

This John Irving was finishing a first novel, as I was, only this John Irving had a wife and two kids, and I had no wife and no kids and haa-haa-haa wasn't I the free little birdy.

After he taught me how to deal with a college grade book, John Irving, the TA (teaching assistant) taught me something else:

"Who are you taking this semester?" he asked.

"I don't know, probably Murray and Yates.

Classes didn't start for another three days.

"You're wasting your time."

"Why, what's wrong with Murray and Yates?"

"Nobody's ever heard of Bill Murray and Yates is on the downslide."

"Then who should I take?"

"Take Vonnegut. Vonnegut's hot right now. You get a rec-ommendation from Vonnegut and editors are going to give your work a serious look."

"But isn't Vonnegut's class filled up?"

"Don't worry. If enough people sign up, they'll add an-other section."

It was a conventional wisdom I'd heard previously around the Workshop – Vonnegut was the guy to go to. Vonnegut was the guy who could help your writing career.

Some silly-minded obstinacy made me stick with Mur-ray and Yates. Murray I liked because there was something pleasant about him; Yates I didn't know very well either but he looked like what I thought a real writer should look like – slightly haggard as if he'd been fighting demons two-thirds of his sleeping hours but emerged strong enough to down a couple of shots, and then hit those typewriter keys. In life and love I'd never been very accurate but I trusted my instincts.

Of course, in the way things work, John Irving was right, as were those other voices in my ear about signing up for the *right* instructor. Another section had to be added for the Von-negut signees and the Writers' Workshop churned on merrily, pretty much like schools anywhere, us hopefuls waiting for a sign from the teacher on just how to proceed and I don't recall a single remark from any of us that would have upset the various groups of burgeoning writers.

This was exactly what *Eleven Kinds of Loneliness* and *Revolutionary Road* warned us about. Life is not about winning or failing, getting published or winning prizes, but somehow finding a harmonious flow the way that river does and that the smile and "wide, shining eyes" of the girl waiting at the top of the library steps isn't just for him – Walter Henderson – it's for all of us for the simple reason that the girl's not a statue, not an emblem of success or failure to be conferred on our dubious manhood; for one brief moment she's a darling little inventor who imagines herself to be a princess in need of rescuing and dear Walter's just the man who will gather her up in his arms and carry her all the way to the river, not in triumph, but to let the quiet and the evening and the river teach them new games. I say this because the river might have told them it wasn't important to hold the title of princess or knight errant but to relax a little, maybe eat a weenie, or just hold hands and listen to the silence.

Hey! Anybody wanna come out and play?

It's not just, as Richard Yates would say, that humans are "inescapably alone"; it's that they "suffer alone." Jean Giono's father said it to him a few days before he died. "The terrible thing is to suffer alone. You will discover that later."

It's not that Richard Yates' fictional characters are so alone; it's that they suffer alone. Walter Henderson cannot tell his wife about his firing because the bridge over the river they have built doesn't carry companionship or friendship or whatever necessary flow that would usher them through the loss of a job. The bridge over the river carries cars, promotions, money belts, check books, tin cans, marriage licenses that say husband and wife, prince and princess, but it doesn't carry the easy-going spiritual attitude that would allow either of them to say, "Great, no job, let's wander the city for a couple of days and just have fun like we used to." And the wife might add on, "Don't worry about the rent. Give me a couple of days to think and I'll help you find a job. We'll work out something. For now, let's have a quiet celebration."

It's a hundred times easier to help someone else than it is to help yourself but usually we get help just at a time when we don't need it. What us apprentice writers 40 years ago at Iowa should have been doing is forgetting our own writing and helping Richard Yates. And if not Richard Yates, then Jean Giono. For it was Giono in at least seven novels, and perhaps more since a lot of his work has never been translated into English, invented characters whose sole purpose is to help other people overcome loneliness. Or, pick the writer of your choice. I can think of at least 15 valuable writers who were out of print in 1967.

The best part is it could have been fun. Three or six people gathered in someone's room or apartment, the drinks flowing, a little food, and innovative ideas being tossed out on just how to get people's attention to Alexander Herzen, or Jules Renard, or Richard Yates. We shouldn't have thought of ourselves as young writers at Iowa in 1967. We should have thought of ourselves as foot soldiers in the service of our masters, the lords and princesses of the written word. It would have called for a whole new way of thinking: about the proper forms to get across to the public the value of certain writers, the value of classrooms, the true cohesiveness of institutional programs in creativity, and simply our role as human beings on this earth. We wouldn't have dared then to call ourselves writers but "caretakers" – mistake-prone people trying, with grace and a sense of humor, to promote what was best and most life-enhancing of the elite in a certain craft.

Who knows where such an approach would have gone. Certainly it would have spared us a lot of Brussels sprouts and might have even healed a few ruptured marriages. It might have helped both ourselves and Richard Yates to realize that before we were writers we were frail little people, wandering out to the avenues at 9 a.m. on a fall Saturday morning. It was sunny and cool and we'd just convinced our parents to buy us a new ball. The trick at that hour was to find somebody to throw the ball to. Even though it was the weekend, parents sometimes had an agenda for their kids, do some yard work, help father wash the car, finish up homework undone from the week before. Sometimes you'd have to stop at four or five open doorways, at each one saying, "Hey! Does anybody wanna come out and play?"

laughter's darkest hour: on rabelais

Since it has reached me via smoke signals from some Indians that the world right now (March 1, 2009) is struggling with its means of getting food and housing – paper currency, I have an idea to save noble humans a lot of aggravation. It is all marvelously simple.

A benign dictator would track down the last 100 people who claimed they laughed out loud while reading François Rabelais. Rabelais was a 16th-century monk who wrote about some giants named Gargantua and Pantagruel who delighted in everything we are told is bad for us – food, drink, sex – and are very happy to be part of the earth. They are also creators; one climbs to the top of the Notre Dame Cathedral, urinates, and creates the River Seine. Yesterday's exaggeration is today's reality. There was no bodily function that the two giants did not relish. They loll in the mud, belch, sing, eat whole boars at a time, fart, dance, and breed every time they get a chance. And everywhere they go there is merrymaking. To inhale the full measure of Rabelais is to start to finally live. Yes, there is work, hard work. But never far away is a party, with tall tales, boisterous laughter, and lutes and flutes. Rabelais restores the body because he finds nothing repugnant about the human body. Any spiritual healing must start with this acceptance. Any sort of fairness, any concept of morality must begin with this notion that the body is the great source of pleasure and all ideas must begin and end there.

Had Rabelais's people and events been any smaller than they were they would have been gobbled up in somebody's philosophical scheme that eventually funneled into The Age of Reason. But as any sane person knows by now, this reasoning succeeded superstition with the logic of a hangman and we are firmly embedded in it. The largesse of Rabelais' world made the powermongers of his time think he was harmless – a mere jokester entertaining himself and a few drunk friends with tall tales. The wily monk had the last laugh.

I would take that laughter a little further. I would have my dictator place the last 100 people who laughed at Rabelais on a large stage. In the pits I would have an orchestra; in the mezzanine the Mormon Tabernacle Choir. Everywhere my dictator would install the latest recording equipment. This might be one of the few instances in modern history where technology works for the health of man. These 100 Rabelaisian laughers would be read a 15- or 25-minute segment. This might be repeated two or three times with other sections of Pantagruel or Gargantua . . . till these listeners issued a really boisterous and prolonged burst of laughter. Between segments the 100 chosen would be given fresh-roasted chicken and a couple of glasses of wine. The orchestra would strike up; the choir would sing, "Hallelujah, hallelujah." Nothing but that.

This scene would not only be broadcast live on television and radio, it would be the only thing to air on those mediums. Computers would be shut down. The next day the same: if anyone turned on the television, radio, or computer they would see/hear only one thing: bawdy laughter at a bawdy story . . . all in praise of the body. Twice a day the actual reading of the various stories that produced this laughter would be aired. In shopping malls, offices, school rooms, car radios there would only be the sound of laughter. Perhaps if a boss or a teacher tried to get back to "business as usual", he would be drowned out with laughter. Recorded or spontaneous from workers or students . . . What's the difference?

This laughter would echo across fields and hills. It would cross oceans and be repeated wherever people were gathering. Even the maimed and the famished would forget their own suffering for a few seconds. The birds would pick up on it and chirp like never before. Cows would stare about baffled, then resume munching their cuds with renewed relish. The streams, the rocks, the trees would all nudge each other, "Look! Humans are laughing. Perhaps there's hope for us."

Even with the most meager resources people would find a way to launch even a small party: some small tidbit to nibble on, something to drink, one of the old songs, a story that puts a smile on the face. Then back to the business of growing food, repairing shelter but with each small success there would be the memory of what eased their considerable burden-laughter.

Laughter is the great purgative. It cleans us out in a way the Ex-lax never can. Free momentarily of what we previously thought were impossible burdens, it is still possible we can come up with ways of surviving without enslaving each other. Laughter suspends belief. We don't need any more beliefs or belief systems. What we need is fidelity to the body; thinking has only helped us dig a hole for ourselves. Laughter creates its own system, a new one where goofiness and serenity sit down side by side holding hands. "Laughter," said the Brazilian writer Jorge Amado, "is the only defense we have against tyranny."

Most of the tyranny is not in political or religious organizations but in our own thinking which makes us raw meat for the tyrant. We race for the protection of the group long before we have come up with anything to add to the group; in this way the group slaps handcuffs around our wrists and we are shackled for life. It has been going on for a long time but now the little jails the various financial and education systems have built are disintegrating and the great panic has started. The problem is not with systems but with each individual. For starters, the individual will find a way to laugh or he will be crushed like a bedbug. It's survival I'm talking about and you'd better grab on to it fast.

The idea of my benign dictator isn't fantastic at all. In the 1960s, an editor of the *Saturday Review* was diagnosed with cancer and told he had one year to live. His name was Norman Cousins and the first thing he did, upon learning this news, was to unplug the telephone. He then instructed his wife to pass meals into his room but otherwise not to disturb him for any reason. Cousins tracked down all his favorite movies and books that had made him laugh and locked himself in his room for the next six months. He watched the Marx brothers, W.C. Fields, Charlie Chaplin, and Buster Keaton. He read Rabelais and other authors. Six months of this fare and he emerged from hiding completely cured.

This little incident alerts us that 99% of our problems are societal ones – the hell that other people make for each other. Unplug our connections to society, listen to the great scoffers and merrymakers and everything will be fine.

People are destroying each other because they don't know how to laugh. I am thinking particularly of the educated and those people known as professionals. Their institutions are dying because for 150 years their bodies have been dead. They don't bleed blood. When their bodies are punctured pus comes out. Sacks of putrefying corpses have been running the show. When they open their mouths to speak gaseous fumes trickle out. We have no language. We have only clacking marionettes using words to put us to sleep while they sneak up on our bank accounts. People who have no guts and no honesty always play a little game with money. It's their one chance to get even in a world that has deprived them of their genitals and clear eyesight. Except on the very edges of civilization there are no men; there are no women. Copulation is a sniveling joke because there is no vitality. Men and women renounced that long ago so they could develop their cunning. Even while they are going through the motions of humping, they are thinking, always thinking of some leverage that lies in store for them. One-upmanship and the emblems of material success but no real exuberance, no real belief in life. Everywhere in the land of skyscrapers I see people yacking away on their wee cell phones but these are only the last whines of a dying race.

Look at the eyes that are attached to the mouths quacking

into these cell phones. They don't take in light and they don't give off light. These are enamel carcasses wired with the latest technology to give the illusion of life. Their flesh hangs from their bones like mounds of afterthought. They are impenetrable and the further they have gotten from life the more their preposterous egos have informed them. Even as their whole way of life is dying, they are hatching ever more preposterous systems of iron-clad logic to redeem their lost assets and their layers of dissipating comfort.

In the press of the West in the last twenty years, a great deal has been made of people growing fat. They quote research that says 50% of the population is now overweight or even obese. What a single voice lacks the courage to say is that none of these fat people had fun getting fat. Their mouths and eyes carry the disdain of a vat of carbolic acid. There have always been fat people, so what. Isn't food fun to eat? Not if you look at the faces of these fat people. Not only have many of them swelled into the grotesque but they've filled up with hatred.

Then gaze into the eyes of those who are not fat. It is the same expression: a guarded cautiousness mixed with distemper, a sense of duty mixed with a wariness of anything from outside that might come between them and that duty. It takes little for it to explode into outright hatred. Of course, this happens regularly with anybody unlucky enough to get too close to them; their children, their mates, their employees, or maybe just the automobile driver who slows down in front of them. Strangers are always fair game for their spleen as long as they are protected behind glass, plastic and metal. Eating or not eating, they don't live in a world that has granted them much physical courage.

Fat, skinny, or muscle-bound, the real issue is not anything that has been talked about in the media. The real issue is how so many people could grow so ugly so fast. Faces are a creation of our spirit and our hands. If we constantly desire to make something not only edible but attractive, chances are our faces will express this desire. The most homely man or woman can be attractive and desirable if they see their mission in life is to be of service. If they see the absurdity of what other people call important, smile brightly at this, and can still manage to construct a life of giving, then they will be downright beautiful. They have not only been true to themselves in the most profound sense, they have fooled God who started them off missing a chin or possessing a nose two sizes too big.

Back in the fourth grade. I and a handful of my cell mates had a marvelous time conferring nicknames on people we observed who were lopsided in one way or another. One kid was christened with the nickname, "Pinhead"; another "Hickle Pickle" because his mother always packed a pickle in his lunchbox and it have him the hiccups. This renaming of people and things lasted all through public school and it bred inventiveness into dozens of other areas. None of it was sanctioned by the authorities.

Humor has nothing to do with what is legal, fair, or respectable. It is always at someone else's expense because deep down humor knows fairness cannot be legislated. Best to have fun with unfairness, incorporate it into the group and into our very bowels to be digested. Now the unfairness of life is part of all our lives, has become hilarity, and frees us for new enjoyments, new tasks. At the moment we laugh, we push some paper currency along the table and yell, "Hey waiter, I'm buying the next round." In his heaven among archangels and flying turds, Rabelais is smiling down at us. Among our fourth grade crew, if a child didn't have a nickname, was addressed formally, he knew it was a way of saying, "You're too uptight, you're dull, go elsewhere."

Imagine then the politician who would run on the platform of putting all the dull people in chains, striped pajamas, and armed with sledgehammers for highway repair. On the backs of their prison uniforms would be the sign, "Dull Person." Motorists, directed to slow down, would lean out their windows, and scream, "Dull Person, Pervert, Suffer!" The suburbs and office buildings in the cities would be emptied. Highways would be calm and easy to drive on. Oil depletion would be at a minimum. Inflation of adjectives . . . like "awesome" would be eliminated. So would these fat, dismal cunts who orchestrate the hiring for companies and institutions, something called "Human Resources". I assure you there is nothing human or resourceful about such departments. Only now the considerable hulks of this most prejudiced of human beings would be wielding pick axes on pavements, laying a new foundation for the road bed.

Onehundred years ago dull people may have dominated institutions but the tentacles of institutions didn't stretch very far. Odd bits of music and language could take root at a local level. Today such vibrations would be funneled into a whole-saler, a distributor, and a million-dollar advertising budget. Technology has done little but strangle the airwaves and re-duce people to nervous apprehension. It has allowed the Dull People to take over and make sure nothing unwieldy got into the mix. It has allowed the Dull People to parade about with titles like "teacher", "writer", "producer", "consultant", "states-man", etc., chanting their tedium and devouring the material resources of the earth, all under the protection of the law and the label of respectability.

Worse, it allowed the Dull People to make sure the sons and daughters of Rabelais led a mole-like existence. It starts in the first quarter of the 20th century with the Queens of the Blues, Ma Rainey and Bessie Smith, who cannot be booked in a theater where whites attend. The prejudice flows in every direction. The nightclub comedian, Lenny Bruce, is arrested 57 times in seven years on a variety of charges including be-ing "irreverent toward the church." Dick Gregory, spokesman through satire for whatever is healthy, is followed by the FBI for 17 years. This in a country that regularly lectures the rest of the world on "freedom of speech." For 27 years, three books of Henry Miller's are banned in Europe and the U.S. on the grounds that they are "obscene." Publishers make millions of dollars from pirate editions while the author runs ads on bookstore bulletin boards asking for "a pair of warm, corduroy trousers." The greatest architect of the 20th century in the U.S. – Frank Lloyd Wright – can't find work for three years because the press has decided he is "immoral" because he divorced his first wife.

The fashions of rigidity change according to the decade but the strangulating climate is always there for those who would do things differently. The great crime of The Dull People has been to squash whatever is excellence, whatever breathes fresh air, is cleansing, pure, and gives hope. They spread their bulbous buttocks and sat on the face of innocence till wherever one looked the atmosphere was one low, mean, vicious common denominator with the twin arches of McDonald's sanctifying the skyline. Death and ugliness everywhere and for those who think otherwise, there's always a policeman in a civilian car waiting around the next bend. And some have the nerve to call it "life."

Hemingway put this in perspective when a reporter asked him what he made of all the manuscripts people were always asking him to read: "People are too prejudiced to write," he told the reporter. It's a significant comment because civilization has now reached a stage of self-indulgence where everyone writes and very few read. It's the last gasp of so-called democracies where everybody's word is as good as anybody else's word. By declaration or inference none of these tomes challenge the systems that have ushered them into being. Behind each manuscript are the usual strangulating *isms* and starched collars of respectability. Not only do people who put words on paper see them as just words, they view them as severed from action. It's just a game, one more separating the body from the flow of language.

What's even worse is that most people are too prejudiced to read. In a U.S. quarterly, a reviewer advises me that Knut Hamsun's *Hunger* could not be published today but he doesn't say why. I know he is right but I also know that what he says of Hamsun is true of Rabelais, Lenny Bruce, Céline's *Death on the Installment Plan*, Miller's *Quiet Days in Clichy*, Terry Southern's *Candy*, Pavel Kohout's *The Hangwoman* and on and on. What might be viewed here as literary hangups extends right into daily conversation and decision making: words are just a way for people to hem themselves in. They don't work at all. Words are just their way of pissing around while the worms wait in the wings to bore a hole in their pancreas. Everywhere walking cadavers.

This is another way of saying that people today expect to be trashed. They don't expect the future to get any better. In their dreams their bodies have told them they are on the wrong path and they can look forward to annihilation. A lot of people are waiting to oblige them, mostly youths who never put much stock in words anyway.

Thus, we can look forward to one of the best parties of the year, a destruction on such a scale that even Rabelais will be cheering from on top of a wine cask in heaven. Perhaps someone will have the forethought to bring a copy to read to the survivors among the rubble. Now people will be free to go "ha-ha-ha". That's the surest sign of a healthy beginning.

on the agent

The Agent by Martin Wagner is a play that reveals through its two snivelling characters why we find people more and more full of shit as we get older. The plot line tells me it is a play about a writer who feels his literary agent has forsaken him but it's really a feverish dialogue on a stage (and now in film form) about why words don't work. When words don't work, we maim each other. Or we drink too much or sniff some sort of plant ground up or in powder form or in pills to get the courage to say what we really think. Neither the agent nor the writer are *on* anything. They are outrageously normal. This is another way of saying both have gone the respectable route. They hold jobs, pay taxes, more or less cohabit with the opposite sex, have been careful not to insult anyone, and when the curtain opens they are pretty much like us – thoroughly miserable. They have been sweet citizens and they are paying the price.

The price is that they use language like a feather duster. Words are a little device to keep the machine clean and greased. As a result, neither the agent nor the writer believe in the tools of their respective trades. The writer isn't sure whether he has written strong books and the agent couldn't tell a good book from a bruised cucumber. Early in the first act, the writer Stephen says to the agent, "You know what sells but do you know what's good?" The agent, Alexander replies, "And what is the difference?"

And lest we blame a breakdown in words on the industry that's supposed to nurture them, the agent quite correctly says, "There are no real readers out there any more. People read to write, or they read to buy, or read to sell . . ."

What has been eliminated here is pleasure. In this case it's the pleasure of reading. But it could be the pleasure of almost anything – growing tomatoes, playing a flute, whistling in the rain, listening to the silence. The implications are constant and enormous in this drama and the implication here is that no one or anything is delicious and fruitful in itself but only in the leverage over other humans which can be gained from it. How often does your telephone ring from a caller who isn't trying to use you for something?

And if we lose the pleasure of living, how long is it before we pick up a gun and shoot someone? This begs the larger question of just how epidemic this loss of pleasure is? And how soon an eruption from nature or from a disgruntled nation will spark an orgy of bludgeoning on the streets?

Martin Wagner's writer also reaches for a gun when he feels words – the tools of his craft, his reason for being – are futile. But as he reaches for his gun, he is quick to inform his agent and us in the audience that the gun is "a metaphorical one." Like everything else. What Stephen in fact has are photographs of Alexander, the agent, and his two secret children whom the agent has never told his new wife about. With evidence of this dastardly secret, the writer blackmails the agent into conducting an auction of his manuscript – the same one the agent thought an hour ago not worth showing to publishers. Better than a dead agent, we have an autopsy, a post-mortem on an industry that's supposed to nurture the best in words to a waiting reader whom we soon learn doesn't exist. The second half of the play/film releases dozens of little truths about the hypocrisy surrounding all language as these two twerps play out their related conspiracies.

What is most amazing about Wagner's play/film is that no one has done it before. Each hour nine writers sprout on every street in Manhattan. In the suburbs of the U.S. and within its vast collegiate system, 136 writers are born each day according to the latest Gallup poll. Now that the U.S. army has burned the poppy fields in Afghanistan the 17-year-old there has only two choices: strap some bombs to his back or write a screenplay for Hollywood. Each year the university system of the United States graduates 6,000 bona fide writers. Bona fide because they have a BFA or an MFA. Bachelors of a Fumigated Asshole, or Masters of a Fumigated Asshole. I have an MFA myself, and I can assure you my turds are less smelly than almost anyone else's on earth.

It has been building up for the last 100 years – this fact now apparent to everyone even mildly interested in formalized language – that everybody is a writer and nobody reads, or reads anything worth reading. The result is a dead language for dead people. Worse, each person thinks his book is just as good as the books that are being published. He thinks he is *entitled* to be published. This means that more forests have to be cut down, more animals displaced, birds sent packing to the edge of the earth. Human vanity knows no limits and though words have been exhausted they are still the mirrors of human worthwhileness. "A vicious circle," you say? Then, why didn't some writer come along before Wagner and dynamite the machinery of his industry?

For two hundred years writers have critiqued every aspect of human endeavor but not the industry that spawns them. To do so for a writer is the same as slitting his own throat. By implication, the French poet Rimbaud does it but his language is so much his own and his vision at age 19 so powerful and fresh that he's been relegated to "comparative literature" departments deep in the bowels of the university. A British writer and a U.S. one did tear into the publishing industry in the 1930s and for their efforts they were banned for the next 30 years. This was D.H. Lawrence and Henry Miller. In the 1960s, the governing stick heads decided Lawrence wasn't so dangerous after all and let weeping coeds and pimpled boys hang around his books. Miller was another story; his words are so infused with a brain-clearing dynamite that he has never gotten on a college syllabus. The teacher would be canned. There are other writers who have hit so close to the nerve endings that their works have been removed from the shelves by publishers. One is Jonathan Kozol and his rich book, *The Night Is Dark and I am Far from Home.* His publisher, Simon & Schuster, took the book from the shelves for several years and then reissued it with a foreword from Kozol which adds up to a Stalinist-type confession. *The Night Is Dark* details how U.S. schools take the sting out of language and any potential heroes or heroines a student might have. Worth also mentioning is Peter Matthiessen's *In the Spirit of Crazy Horse.* It was released by Viking Press right after a shootout in the 1970s by a rebellious segment of the Sioux Indians and the FBI. And almost immediately plucked back off the shelves by Viking . . . and 18 months later reinstated in bookstores. Neither writer wanted to discuss the bannings with me, Matthiessen by mail, Kozol in person. Both are alive, both survive by their writing.

Of the above writers, only Miller tackled the writing industry head on in essays published in obscure journals. These were later collected for books published by Barney Rosset and James Laughlin, readers turned publishers with as much guts and discernment as their best writers. The other three writers I've mentioned hacked away at the rotten pillars of respectable society but stopped just short of dissecting their own industry. Miller lived long enough to see not only the country of his birth but most of what we call civilization unravel through wars, colonialism, street protests, and rebellious music. The vacuum in power was partially filled with dozens of writers more daring than their predecessors and world use of words in theater, film-making, poetry, novels, and most of all in music had a downright giddy vibrancy from 1957 through 1980.

By 1985, the banks and military had recovered their leverage. Educational institutions and publishers sniffing profits galore soon got in line. That word "art" and that word "culture" could be used to sell almost anything. Prize money for haikus and the best design for a new rollercoaster spilled on to the streets. Kids in the colleges decided poetry wasn't so difficult after all and could be used for vital self-expression and to get ahead with their budding careers. The deans obliged them and charged appropriately. The mere sound of the word "creative" was a mental aphrodisiac. Ohh to be an artist and be loved and make money at the same time. You could have just about everything and have it all at once and everywhere all over your itchy-gitchy, ooey-gooey chum-chum bod. Why life was easy. Didn't all the guidebooks and self-help books and marketing books say so? Just hang back, keep it cool, obey your superiors, and look for the right connections. Mother was right when she said, "It's not what you know but who you know."

If the hierarchy of what was excellence in the old forms had been pushed aside, a new hierarchy took its place – middle men to usher the product – soup spoons or novels – to a flush and waiting public. The idea was that middlemen – brokers of one sort or another – could take the pressure off of the makers of products and allow them more time and freedom to perfect their product. In reality what happened was the sellers dictated to the makers the kind of product they were to make . . . if they wanted to survive. In the case of words whether ferreted out in books, in classrooms, through the media, all language within 20 years became the language not of making but of marketing.

In the case of books, little bookstores and little publishers were gobbled up by corporations, none of them particularly concerned about the vitality and truthfulness of words, only which words could rake in the dough. Since all institutions felt obliged to offer some sort of plan and often apology for what they were doing, they soon picked up on this marketing language. A school, a company, a government agency was only as good as the language it used to convince the public, or at least its stockholders, that it was doing good. "Good" might be in service to a given constituency but more often this notion of good could be fudged aside with a heady list of abstractions built around "progress", "competition", "getting ahead", "team work", "discipline", etc. etc. till words didn't identify any sort of reality but functioned to obscure it. One corporate prospectus read like another; an English department course syllabus was the same in South Dakota as it was in Alabama. Language wasn't aimed at the people you were supposed to be serving but toward your superiors who would pass it on to their superiors, all to increase the battle shield around the all-governing institution.

Somehow, coincidentally, the human body bloated and broke down at the same time words broke down. Food and words had their connection to any kind of roots in place and time severed. Just as the U.S. printed money when it ran short, we'd invent reality as we went along. The result was that prisons, drug-treatment centers and nut houses filled up and more are being built as I write. Right across the earth it was a landscape of lies; the earth itself buckled and heaved as more lies were tossed out each day. In the West, people got more and more money but where could they spend it? The food sources were poisoned. Healthful water came in bottles but no one was sure where that water came from. The so-called entertainment, for those on earth who could afford it, was little more than delirious babble. In several thousand years of "civilization" no one had learned anything except that refrain of mothers through the ages about hanging out with the right crowd.

None of this is new. It has happened repeatedly throughout history, most recently in 1945 when the earth woke to try to recover itself among debris and rubble in the cities and 65 million people dead and the survivors in a state of shock from which we've never recovered but rather passed on to our children and grandchildren a set of dreary *isms* and ologies, all with the design of insulating a certain in-group at the expense of the non-believers. To be a person, something called a "human being", is a disaster, a non-entity, which has made the earth uninhabitable for other species.

The answer of course to all this debacle is to go online. Then when you are done, say, "Awesome." And everything will be fine.

The Agent, this play by Martin Wagner, wasn't performed at The Old Red Lion Theatre, London on March 6th, 2007; it was performed at the edge of the Moon in the year zero. Its cast got a pittance in remuneration for the art they believed in and executed in a skillful fashion. Anyone who really believes in the product that they are making doesn't get paid on this earth in the year 2008. Money goes to the liars and thieves.

The writer, Wagner, had to put on the play with his own money, print the book with the play with his own money, and then with the little he had made, execute a film version which is now about to enter film festivals in Europe and the U.S.

That he had to do everything himself is not news. In the U.S., Thoreau and Whitman had to self-publish; Emily Dickinson's poems were found in a desk drawer after her death. And these writers are considered the foundation of U.S. literature. Yet he has not gone the success route, which is to say the route of existing machinery, so this play which alerts us to the travesty that has become language has only been reviewed in a few media outlets. The words "self-published" are just as much of a stigma now as 150 years ago.

Yet *The Agent*'s total clarity about the hole we've gotten ourselves into through the use of words signals in this age of calculated cowardice the play had to be put on by the writer himself. The established literary czars wouldn't have the guts to produce it or see it into book form.

It's about a great deal more than a writer trying to find out from his agent if his writing is worthwhile or even marketable. It's about anybody who is trying to find out through the eyes and words of others if he has any value. The very nature of anything creative revolves around the making of something new. But if this newness can only be translated in terms of the money it brings in, how do we know it is new? Marketing mostly revolves around proven formulas. The seeker of self-worth is strapped into an absurdity, a meaningless existence.

In the meantime, we will all pretend. And pass these

pretenses – these masks of hopelessness on to our children whom we advise to honor all existing systems lest they lose their footing, not "get ahead", forfeit "security", are out of tune with "progress", even as those same children watch the world crumbling around them in war and chaos.

These pretenses begin in the play with the agent, Alexander, fumbling for considerable time with the connection to his computer. He has to get under the desk to try to get it working. That is where his client, Stephen, finds him when he enters the office. It is a message we are all alerted to by age seven: it is not people but the machinery of control we have to plug in to.

Still under the desk, Alexander is queried by Stephen in a naive hopeful voice, questions that become a pattern throughout the play and probe at the very nature of his agent's business. He asks if the agent has read all the books he sees on the shelves?

"They're our authors."

Stephen: "Just for fun?"

Alexander: "I read first drafts, tenth drafts, outlines, synopses, whatever. The finished books? (shrugs his shoulders) There just isn't time."

But Stephen is neither naive nor hopeful. He's an actor, playing out a string. The string is attached to the metaphorical gun in his briefcase. So, most of his questions are rhetorical; he has a good idea of the answers or the fact that to many of his questions his agent, his benefactor is going to do an elaborate waltz. The fun for him, and for the audience, is watching the agent squirm. Lies, evasion, hypocrisy are the order of the day, as they are in our own lives. The agent makes no more sense than the 50 advisors, teachers, brokers we've had in our own lives.

But because Stephen is skillful enough to keep backing him up and eventually corner him, we also get revelations, not just about the writing industry but the fate of what constitutes excellence. Worse, we get a sense that occasionally Alexander does fathom what is quality, not just saleability.

Twenty minutes into the play, the agent, by way of hinting he no longer wants Stephen, tells him a story about the trouble a colleague had with a writer she no longer wanted to represent.

"She just hated *them* (his books) . . . But every spring, like clockwork, the new manuscript landed on her desk. Every year it was a little longer, a little heavier, a little more *worthy* (italics mine), and a little more unpublishable. She dreaded every new book."

But just ten minutes earlier, the agent had advised Stephen, "All great writers make it sooner or later."

This latter phrase is part of the "conventional wisdom" of book publishing. I heard it 40 years ago at the University of Iowa. In case I forgot it, I got a reminder of it April 8th, 1994, from Robert Loomis of Random House. Loomis is still the operations head in the U.S. of the largest publishing company in the world. Loomis writes, "My perception is that there are very few good books that don't get published."

Book publishing is comparatively new. Five hundred years ago we had lore or mythology, passed word-of-mouth to tell us about the possibilities within ourselves to finding connections with other people, the superiority and usefulness of nature, the suggestion of other horizons where we might find greater pleasure and harmony if only we dared to take the first step and put aside some of our old ways of thinking. Words in the form of poems, theater, stories always had to do with the rediscovery of life itself. It had to be this way because humans have always been tormented by the fact that they are going to die. A profitable time on earth might be looking for the sort of companionship that could entertain us through songs, stories, mime, dancing puppets, pictures with color and movement, masks that imitate our demons, all of them ultimately stripping monsters of the power that immobilized us and freeing us to find other forms of survival and pleasure.

But the forms of survival get so speeded up that words

cannot keep up with them, language loses its elasticity; humans are frozen in terror; they fall for all sorts of things that are labeled consumable but are simply a series of lies. What is called consumable clogs up the arteries, rivers, seas, atmosphere, eats with its acids the coral reefs, the lungs, and brain. Then words become a poor excuse for people gone amuck.

Much of the play is about this speed. Speed adds up to money. The agent, in five hours, auctions Stephen's novel, and the promise of two others, for £250,000.00. It was a book that took the author several years to write. He has been waiting several months for his agent, Alexander, to make a decision on its worthiness. The play is divided between Stephen's detailing of the anxiety during this waiting process and Alexander's comic efforts to conceal the fact that he doesn't want the book nor Stephen. At other times Alexander's euphemisms indicate that he doesn't know the book, may have only glanced at it.

Wagner has adopted an interesting little device for the agent to deal with his client's questions. He has him hesitate and then pounce on a word as if he's just discovered it. For example, the agent offers a cliché about his role, "After all, that's what I'm here for. To cut out the dead wood..."

Stephen: "Dead wood?"

Alexander: "You know I like your writing. It's . . . *interesting* (italics, author's). There are just a few things that are too... *clever.*"

And it's not just the agent. All humans who would assume power over us are on a fishing expedition on just how to use words to have them maintain leverage over us. They use words to quietly slide the door shut, not to open the door to let in light. These agents of our goods and our sense of self-importance fasten themselves to the symbolic function of language. One hundred and ten years ago newspaper editors, glancing over their shoulder at the leaders of industry, branded striking workers "anarchists" without defining the term or its strings to local conditions or a particular group of people.

The word "anarchist" could not only be all-encompassing but it could cause fear. Its counterpart today might be "terrorists", "militants" or someone who is "unprofessional." The mere mention of this on an individual's personal record can send him drifting to the end of the continent to make a living. George Orwell has a brilliant essay on this kind of language in "Politics and the English Language".

For certain this is a short-cut language to make us believe we know something when we really don't. It is the idiom of people in a hurry. Its goal is not just material wealth but some thing far more insidious – belonging to a group out of fear of being alone. The agent belongs to a loose and shifting fraternity of other agents and editors: he's part of an industry, one which doesn't make anything but arbitrates what can be disseminated.

The writer on the other hand works alone. Unless he is very successful, he will have little contact with the vast industry that supports him. Periodically he may meet with other writers but chances are they will talk about the business end of their profession, about the industry that has little need for most of them. This aloneness leads a writer like Stephen to all sorts of miscalculations about the nature of his talent and how it might be received. Stephen realizes this when he says to Alexander, "But you were finally able to take out an hour and read it. At the end of the conversation I feel amazed that I have such a wonderful agent, someone who actually takes the time to read my stuff. You ask me to come for a meeting. I'm so flattered to get a call from you at all, that when I put the phone down, that I realize you haven't said what you think."

A good third of the play is about the world of self-doubt and hopefulness of the writer. It is the rebellion against this hopefulness that Wagner paints through Stephen. His is in an entirely different world than the agent. His admission here is a reminder, too, to the non-writer that we all live in a world where very few people say what they think. Just as bad, it's hard to find anybody who does what they say. And worse still, we are all trained that way – words are just this silly game we play for our superiors or when we want something from someone. Reality belongs to the people who hold the guns. The threat of the gun at someone's head is just as valuable as pulling the trigger. Men and women, children and dogs live in a world of coercion. Stephen, the writer, decides to drop words and get in on the fun. He takes some photos and blackmails his once theoretical benefactor, making him a real benefactor.

What gets lost in this sort of language are our ears and eyes. Words aren't connected, as they once were in primitive society, to what we have heard, seen, touched, smelled. For this minor function of pleasure and language we have machines. In Wagner's world, generalizations don't have to be rooted to the senses or in example; Words like "interesting", "clever", "passive" float in space all by themselves, disconnected from locale, trees, nerve endings. We are in a world of delirious and heady abstraction, a lot like our daily lives. What we have for replacement is a lot of jangled wiring – computers, faxes, telephones, intercom systems, speakerphones. In this dazzling and dazed world the conversations between Stephen and his agent are like our own daily talk – a lot of meaningless gibberish. Aren't we a breath away from the catchall word, the fabulous calling card of our age? "AWESOME" the cry goes up. In the feverish lips of the young this might describe a date the night before or some idiot's first day at a new job; it might describe the flavor of doughnuts or the hole in the doughnut at the local coffee shop. And everybody nods as if they know perfectly well what the word means. And we wonder why there is violence?

This sets up a massive vacuum in the guts of the living. This hole in the stomach has always been there. It happens when this creature called a human being climbs down from the tree, stands upright on two legs, looks about and realizes he is going to die. If not tomorrow, then in a few years, and wonders how his brief time on earth should be spent, after he has slept and breakfasted on some nuts and berries. In a feverish gibberish the apemen bat this around for awhile till one of their troop, one of the more thoughtful and patient apemen, steps forward and says in tree-talk, "Slow down, don't give in to fear, let's work this out."

Words when they are used well keep humans from just flailing at the notion of non-existence, total darkness, inertia, immobility, with not a hint of how we might move. Sometimes it's not even words but a series of clicking, chirping sounds in imitation of the insects and birds to indicate the delight we take in moving, having voices, feeling desire in our hands and foreheads.

Or it might be a prolonged moan to indicate loss, loss of a child, a husband, a mother. Someone else picks up on this moan, extends it; two others pull the moan back down – the first blues song, the beginning of not giving in to death, inertia, the status quo, something new to indicate death will not win. It might be called regeneration. Or even resurrection, except that it happens on earth, before our eyes and ears.

All else is gibberish, a capitulation to anxiety. Creativity is not something for the more talented, the college-bound dolts. It's for everyone, at all times. It should be the very air we breathe. It will grow of its own accord; it need not be nurtured by institutions: institutions have attached creativity to group belonging which meant more and more rules for validation and ultimately strangled the song or poem. And if the songs and poems don't work for us, we destroy the world around us. The old emptiness has taken over.

Wagner is very alert on how we try to fill this emptiness. Bluff! This is another word for ego or self-importance. Even as the agent, Alexander, is being blackmailed into auctioning a product he thinks unworthy but may not even know, he delights in the game – in the process. He even rebels at the idea that Stephen, five hours into his blackmailing scheme, wants to pull out. "You can't do that," he barks at Stephen. "Why? I thought you'd be happy. You're off the hook." "Don't you get it? This is not about you any more." "It isn't?" "It's me who is on the line here; not you, me. What do you think my 'chums' will do to me if they find out about this?" "That's your problem. I'm out of here." "Like it or not, we're in it together now. I have my reputation to protect."

It's not merely that Alexander would be flushed from the group if the blackmail was discovered but the process by which the literary industry funnels words to a waiting public would be seen as fraudulent.

In real life there have been such exposures. Around 1973, an aspiring writer took Jerzy Kosinski's *Steps*, a novel which had won the National Book Award a couple of years earlier, and had it typed up, put his name on it, and mailed it to Kosinski's publishers, Houghton & Mifflin. Two months later he got the following reply, "Your writing shows great promise. But I, and a number of other editors, feel that the characters must be more fully developed before the novel could be considered for publication. Furthermore . . ."

Of course, the aspiring writer took his story to the media and they gobbled it up. Grinning like a mongoose still in heat, he appeared on all the talk shows and became a hero to a million other aspiring writers. He did not make a career of writing. There would be other similar tricks played on the publishing industry but he was the first. It has culminated in a system where a writer has no hope of reaching a commercial publisher without an agent. The agent's the guy who screens out these characters clever enough to reveal an industry that has no idea what it is doing.

Beyond money and group belonging, Alexander's ego has a third component, The Deal. If money is the artifact that keeps all the gears greased, The Deal is the agent's one chance to wheel and deal, invent out of thin air, do what the writer does – make something out of nothing. As an interesting appendage to Stephen's deal, Alexander lies about the identity of the author. He tells prospective publishers the author is a "great-looking woman." The playgoer or reader should feel right at home. He knows that whether you are pushing a candy bar or the weather on the nightly news you need a woman's handsome face because attached are a pair of mammaries. It's okay, even advantageous, if the weather woman has cleavage, but not too much, not too precipitous or we might forget all about cloud cover and try to suckle the plastic screen. In a sexless society you need all the symbols of sex you can get to make them buy things.

Alexander defines The Deal, alias the modern ego: "It's like an addiction. You just can't get enough. The book's the first step, of course, but once it's gone out the door, the deal is all that matters. I just love waiting while they (publishers) try to figure out what I want."

The Deal is having something other people want but have some difficulty figuring out what they have to offer to get that something. Money is only part of it. It can also be control over presentation, over ownership of the film rights, specifics of how the book is to be marketed, paperback distribution. Quality certainly isn't part of The Deal; it is irrelevant. As Alexander says, "Once the book is out the door, it takes on a life of its own." That life is a marketing life with marketing language. It is no different than our bread or beer which may or may not have genuine wheat, or hops and barley in it. By the energy level of the people I've glimpsed in the U.S. and Europe, I would say that they're not being fed very well.

There is no doubt in my mind that the various civilizations are frozen in their forms and languages. I see this in the disdain the average person carries in his face and the absolute fear around the earth of the stranger. Yet I can also remember a time when the poor and people of modest means were quite open to the stranger – the outsider, the different one, the potential catalyst for something new. I can also remember a time when agents weren't necessary and publishers didn't feel they had to make a killing with every book they signed up. Ten percent of the books they published each year would be by new writers. Some of these new writers dove into content and places that hadn't been touched before; others stretched form till it coughed up new kinds of logic and hinted at new ways of living. It was all new. Regardless, there was room for them till they built up a body of work and attracted a few thousand readers. As an example I can remember Knopf publishers printing a book of B. Traven's and one of Jean Giono's novels in the 1950s. Both of them had world followings but neither writer's work caught on in the US. But at least old man Knopf had tried, and the lesson to other generations of writers was that there was at least one publisher in the U.S. who understood what excellence was.

No such publisher exists today. The notion of a publisher adopting a custodial approach with a tiny portion of his output has disappeared. Small independent publishers and occasionally a university publisher will try to make up the slack but without distribution there is little they can do. The problem is more than just corporate giants squeezing out the little guy but a deterioration of language until it has become gibberish in every corner of the globe.

Wagner's miracle is that he has identified the gibberish and woven it in a way that identifies the nature of the enemy. Hopefully, this play will start something: a few thousand young people, or young writers, will no longer be terrified by the word "success". They may realize that their teachers of writing and literature are just as full of shit as this agent Wagner created. They may even give up the notion of writing. Then look out. They just might take up new, and more profitable careers. As to what I'm not going to say. But I'll be sitting in the wings, ready to coach them on their new career.

what i would tell young writers

The first thing I would say to the young writer is take the pressure off. By pressure I mean making writing serve some ulterior purpose: getting a grade, winning a prize, impressing a teacher or editor, or convincing a potential mate of his talent. Talent is everywhere; believable language is now (2008) almost nonexistent. Most writing is conceived and executed with an advisor looking over the writer's shoulder. And yet there is not a teacher or writer or parent or anyone who understands the role of the written word. Young writers – in any country – have been so thoroughly coerced that the written word is dead. The educators and publishers have seen to that. But every other facet of life has cooperated.

Yes, we "live" in a world of the dead and the dying. This was also true in 1946 but with one important distinction – a lot of people were congratulating themselves at still being alive.

And that is what someone who hopes to make sense to other humans will have to do – congratulate himself at being alive. The next step is for the would-be writer to find a way to feel himself beautiful and brave. To do this, he may have to walk to the very edge of civilization, peek over the edge, and jump. If he lands on his feet, or even must crawl, he will find himself behind the mirror. Never again will an editor's applause or rejection have much effect on him. He has sat in the weeds, wandered through jagged vines, smelled mud, drifted up all sorts of mysterious trails, become acquainted with himself for the first time.

Was it not the composer and pianist Liszt, who upon receiving a request from a young lady for piano lessons, said, "Go out and live for five years. Then come back and advise me that you still want piano lessons." It was Liszt's way of saying that music is not some virtuoso technique but an extension of life itself.

Liszt was also saying that to make art the woman must first learn how to live. The young writer will realize he is well on the way of learning how to live if he wakes all excited morning after morning. This enthusiasm may take the form of writing a short story or it may translate into a walk around the block and the world will not be worse off for not having one more short story.

To learn how to live, the would-be writer must make himself deliciously lazy. He should stay in bed as long as possible. And if he insists on getting out of bed, dawdle somewhere – in the bath tub, at the kitchen table, under a tree. What is important is that he not do anything; certainly he shouldn't try to prove his merit on this earth. Above all, he should stay away from words – his own or anyone else's. If he has the phenomenal luxury of looking out on a scene of beauty – the ocean or the forest, or perhaps only a tree in his backyard – he ought to gaze on it for long time. A cup of tea or coffee is a fine lubricant for appreciating the morning but not too much. Let the juices distill, allow the eyes and ears to concentrate on what is right in front of them. Tune out the mind. Stretch the legs and arms. Remind the self that it is unimportant. Ask what sorts of heroes will be born today in a bird's nest or a rabbit's den.

There are all sorts of advantages to lazy beginnings. Heroes arise in blades of grass or a drunken uncle no one talks about. Duty takes a furlough. Anything practical that first hour of the morning is regarded as obnoxious. A demanding pet is a pest. Best of all is the discovery that busyness is a disease of Western Civilization. It probably grew out of that "quiet desperation" that Thoreau talked about among his neighbors in Concord, Massachusetts. This comes from the abiding inner awareness – this desperation – that we aren't living our lives at all. It has as its greatest ally – respectability. For anyone who wants to live, or write, there is no greater enemy than this solemn couple called busyness and respectability.

Such beginnings will remind our fledgling writer of the marvelous supremacy of silence and that most of the words he hears on a given day are nothing more than impotent buzzing. He will accumulate these silences, learn to love them, and they will reward him with a deep inner calmness.

Most importantly, the human hoping to make contact with the world through words will not greet the day with an argument. This is fatal. Of course there's plenty to confront but it's been that way for a long time and a young writer should realize he's a creator, not a reformer. In conception and execution, what we call civilization is 99% wrong. It is not Frank Lloyd Wright or Mahatma Gandhi who have been emulated but the latest fashion which in itself is a cover up for expediency and dollar. It is all dying. Best to let it expire as quietly as possible.

All I have said so far is little more than a reminder that the writer is on his own. Most of what is called "literature" or the "classics" is nothing more than the fashion of a certain age. Most of the writers heralded 10 or 20 or 50 years ago have no use. Before he invented the Nobel Prize, Nobel invented dynamite. All the prizes could use a little of his first product.

By now the would-be writer has taken his first steps toward freedom. He can accelerate this apprenticeship by walking away from all that he has known and taking a good look at something different for an extended period of time – the forests, a new country, a village whose people bear no resemblance to previous creatures he has known. If he doesn't have a language to communicate with these new creatures, so much the better. He can substitute mime which will do the job if his spirit is open enough and gracious enough. Otherwise, he may have to take up residence in some cannibal's cooking pot. The latter could prove an expedient way of burning off false ego – that résumé existence – that formerly gave him his identity.

Because the U.S. and most of what is called "civilization" has cornered currency which means survival, the would-be writer will have to return to a world of gadgets and wires and ferocious traffic. This means a return to the hell of the cities. If he didn't fit before in an insane, conveyor-belt existence, he will be driven half mad by his encounter with it again and his attempts at mere survival for the third or fourth time. It is now, in the daily whine of ambulance sirens and screech of car tires, he must summon the detachment born at the edge of the forest or along the seashore. Quickly he will see that all that is called "culture" or "civilization" is a euphemism for exploitation, cruelty, absurdity, and a mass march toward suicide. The cities and towns, computers and newspapers, concert halls and schools aren't anything. In the same breath he should realize this is old news; Balzac and Tolstoy, Gogol and Whitman were talking about it 150 years ago. People don't fathom. They don't get anything . . . until it is too late. There is little to be done about them. No amount of elucidation is going to penetrate that wall they have built around their hearts and skulls with words. In a word, they are terrified of existence and recoil at anything – especially words – that is life-enhancing. The alert would-be writer already knows that humans are going to slaughter each other the way they have destroyed everything else.

But rather than an occasion for regret, the would-be writer will rejoice. He has been outside the circle, sampled real life, found a way to delight in his brief existence. He knows he must savor those strands of words that let the light trickle in and quiet himself so that he and a few kindred spirits can build a new life on the ruins of the old. In his few spare moments, he may consult any number of writers who evoked the only thing worth evoking – the miracle of human personality and its counterpart in nature among the trees and rocks, animals and birds. There is nothing else: the peculiarity of place matched to the amazing and odd variety of humans. I am thinking of Cossery, Voinovich, da Cunha, H. Miller, Traven, Asturias, Rulfo, Sherwood Anderson, and many others. But the would-be writer can make his own list. His apprenticeship in writing is now ready to blossom and won't be with his own creativity but rather the creativity of others. He will be a foot-soldier for those writers he believes in. He may write essays on such writers, post signs in bookstores, on telephone poles on the sides of waste cans. He will do everything possible to get attention to his favorite writers, often dead and no longer able to defend themselves.

This is only my way of saying what Bohumil Hrabal of the Czech Republic told me one afternoon 15 years ago: "We are all a link in a chain. I could never have written without the help of 20 or so other writers including your namesake, James Joyce." Hrabal, though he was severely persecuted by both Nazi and Communist authorities, found a way to keep writing and keep celebrating till the day he jumped out of a hospital window in Prague.

By taking up the banner of Hrabal and other necessary writers, the would-be writer will participate in W.H. Auden's brilliant line, "Teach the free man how to praise." It was originally written on behalf of W.B. Yeats, yet 700 years ago the black pygmies of the Congo River were beginning their day by singing the praises of the forest and its animals. Not many of their songs make it into college anthologies. Even their neighbors, the Bantu-speaking people, regard them as inferior yet unlike the Bantu, and most of us, they have never gone to war.

It was also in Africa, in the early 20th century, that novelists developed the habit of leaving their books on a tree stump for the first person who came along. The would-be writer will have to learn to do this also or develop his own form of divorcing his writing at some stage from the preposterous ego that started the whole enterprise. Without such an apprenticeship that shapes disinterest, the would-be writer will find himself like Chaplin's bolt tightener in *Modern Times* trapped in the gears and subject to experiments like automatic feeders.

what great writers did for me

I awoke this morning grateful to so many writers who put a smile on my face for so many years. I was thinking of them altogether and I didn't have any particular one in mind. What exactly they did for me I didn't focus on either except that they were guides suggesting a direction rather than a specific place, hints of how to be rather than a specific course of action, amiable buddies sniffing out the landscape as opposed to cultural directors who thought they had the truth. The most valuable of them had made me laugh; others suggested the limitless terrain words are capable of creating; then there was Euclides da Cunha of Brazil casually noting the noble heroism of the poorest and most desperate of his characters. Each had an area where they glowed like the brightest star and made me move more lightly as I went out to the avenues.

I am thinking of Alexander Herzen, B. Traven, Vladimir Voinovich, James Herlihy, Sherwood Anderson, Carson McCullers, Karen Blixen, an Iranian writer named Behrangi, a Turk named Hikmet, César Vallejo, Eric Lawlor, Bruce Chatwin, Jean Giono, Albert Cossery, Henry Miller, Eduardo Galeano, Juan Rulfo, Nikolai Gogol, Flannery O'Connor, Buchi Emecheta, Terry Southern, Nelson Algren, Miguel Asturias, José Donoso, Ferdinand Céline, Manuel Puig, Jules Renard, Charles Bukowski, Alan Sillitoe, Eugéne Ionesco, Edward Albee, Cabrera Infante, Alejo Carpentier, Harold Pinter, Charles Bukowski, Bohumil Hrabal, Pavel Kohout, a Pole named Borowski, Bruno Schulz, Elias Canetti, Aimé Césaire, a historian named Arcinieagas, Jorge Amado, Pablo Neruda, a New Orleans poet named Maddox, a New York poet named Stettner, James Baldwin, Richard Wright, Ralph Ellison, Nikki Giovanni.

Some of the above only had a story or a few poems that

fascinated me. Others, like Giono, made me hang on their every word. All of them arrived, like the U.S. Cavalry, just in the nick of time to save me from the enemy – dullness and dread which was all around me. To the list above I am sure I could add another thirty names tomorrow.

What they all have in common is that they inspired me to think life worth living. It had nothing to do with my own writing. No, it was more like they taught me how to see and hear. This was especially true in what is called "Western Civilization." Once out of it, living my life for weeks and months at the edge of the sea, or in various forests and rainforests, I had little need of them. Then, the wind, trees, small animals tried to teach me to see and hear.

But I don't have the advantage of living in a secluded area of nature right now. I am forced to live for the moment in U.S. civilization with all its attendant denial of life and I suppose it was for that reason I've begun thinking of the debt I owe so many good writers and what they did for me.

The word I want to feast on is "inspiration" and just how those writers excited that word in me. After a particular phrase I would feel a gladness at the base of my spine that would both quiet me and give me hope that life could be different. Often it would be sufficient to make me quit my own writing for at least a week. During that time I had only to really listen to Céline or Miller or whoever I happened to be reading. So, if I stumbled across a phrase I really liked, it was important for me to step and inhale the phrase. It wasn't just the meaning of what I was reading; it was the music of it. Then I would have to distance myself from it, go to the window and light a cigarette, maybe reheat the coffee, tiptoe back to it the way you would approach a potentially dangerous animal. To take the full measure of the sentence or paragraph, I'd read it aloud, softly. No sense getting too rambunctious. Then I'd move back from the book again, let the music of what I'd just read work on me. For me it was important not to analyze it. Just let it work on me till it penetrated my pancreas and sometimes my balls. Certainly the people I read I didn't want to appreciate; I wanted them to become a part of me. And it wasn't anything like "literature" I was dealing with – that word means nothing to me – but hints of a whole new world, a new way of being that if I were lucky I might convert to my own new world some day.

I am always amazed how I can return to certain writers 10 or 20 years after I have first read them, open their books in the middle, and feel that I'm not only returning to a conversation with an old friend but the quiet glee I feel at just one of their phrases. Yesterday I opened Céline's *Journey to the End of the Night* at page 118 and heard, "When not actually busy killing, your soldier's a child." Such a sentence was enough to fortify me for the day against all the hopeless ugliness this suburb has constructed to guide me down the highway.

Céline's line was a reminder that wherever we pick up the thread of such an author, they give off light. As they wrote, they were not following a prescription, but a light deep inside them. Words then became not a way of defining, not a method for demarcating but a way of inching the body toward the light. I can easily imagine it as a pair of hands pushing aside the darkness to let in the light. That light is little more than being part of a life force and enlarging both ourselves and whatever we touch. It means we are guests not rulers and wherever we move we had better make room for other creatures. And if we grow taller and stronger, it's not because we are superior but are merely blossoming to fill out a certain role.

A big chunk of that role is the delight we take in being alive and our faith that we can enjoy ourselves no matter where we are. This may mean talking to our toes or picking our nose. It has little to do with meaning and thought is mostly peripheral to enjoyment.

It seems simple enough but try finding it among a group of 18-year-olds in a classroom. This is an institution called "college" and in the year 2008 most U.S. youngins have been persuaded this is a direction they ought to head. And they look just like me when I was 18 years old: dazed, drifting, awaiting the next order that will get them out of the cold and into a warm room. By age seven they've been persuaded to hand over their lives to the next available expert. The same as was going on 500 years ago. And as everybody knows, we can find three available experts on any street corner.

I venture into these collegiate disaster areas every two or three years because I am broke and I can't do anything that is useful to society. It's a soft gig. I write some gibberish on the board and the little idiots scribble it down and then three weeks later vomit it up for some test. This is called "progress" and they are "getting ahead." In a capitalist society these are my suckers and I'm running a scam. People suffer at my expense and I get paid for it. My students go on to become useful members of society while I retire to South Borneo to fart in peace. It takes three to five months to get civilization out of your system after you've been in it for a while.

The clunker comes when I tell these goggling acolytes they are free to write about whatever they want. (This is called a "composition" course.) Then I take it a step further. I commit the sacrilege of sacrileges: I suggest they write about something that gives them pleasure. Heads look up at me with a faint smirk on their cheeks as if I have just told them a dirty joke about their grandmother. Two or three – usually the brighters ones – look relieved. But there is always one who falls out of his seat into the aisle and begins to thrash. The eyes really glaze over and his arms and legs dart in all directions as if he's warming up to take his place in a pinball machine. I instruct the students to ignore him; the first onslaught of freedom always has its casualties.

For six or eight weeks we sail along merrily, the kids writing about some little nugget that has kept them entertained. Curiously, it's usually an activity – skateboarding, piano playing – that in some way reminds them of the joy and freedom of living; rarely do other people figure in this bit of happiness they've carved out. And where other people enter to contribute to their happiness, it's hard for them to assess the nature of this contribution. A deviant uncle hops along an area of street vendors in Bogota, Colombia, picking up debris and singing to himself but he never gets beyond being a bit of an eccentric, a curiosity, acceptable but never penetrated as to the nature of his mystery.

Somewhere toward the end of the semester, the institution reclaims its territory: late papers and the "research" paper arrive looking like they were churned out by an impersonal machine. These events and this information resemble a massive arrow bolting across the sky, independent of human aspiration, desire, or satisfaction. It's like the rest of the student's life – out there somewhere beyond him but ultimately controlling him and demanding his allegiance: computers make for progress, as does stem-cell research and triple-bypass operations, rats for research, and people for better and better feeding. Something like that. And if I'm not exactly accurate, it's because I've fallen asleep, or gone out for a beer after the third paper. I've had dozens of writers take me to the top of the mountain with words and there is no reason I have to tolerate this diarrhetic sludge of dismal mediocrity.

Such papers looked like planks that have lain in the rain for the past month. They are packed with information, every other line imbued with meaning, the whole of it draped in a massive black curtain of crises. Of course, the student doesn't believe a word of it; it's just gibberish he puts down to be rewarded with a symbol that will keep him out of the cold and in front of a teevee which will give him the additional reward of more gibberish along with the admonition to get his ass out to the avenues and buy some plastic shit.

It's the sort of language the student hears everywhere: from preachers and priests, teachers and journalists, parents and well-meaning friends. Its two major components are complaint and a crisis. This is the same as the experts were sounding 500 years ago when priests competed with each other to see who could get the most angels on the head of a pin. Complaint and a crisis can only be overcome through a reward from the people announcing the crises; a grade, job promotion, a bag of M&M candies, anything that will put a buzz in his head before it is lopped off. If he hops after the buzzes fast enough, he can even burn off his own personality like the bushmen along the Kalahari Desert who set fire to the savannah so the animals are deprived of cover to hide from hunters.

Now I am beginning to sound like there is a crisis. But there isn't a crisis. There never was and never will be.

I say this because I forgot to mention a young lady in one of my classes. She is that one in 20, or one in 500,000 who walks to the beat of a different drummer. On her papers her syntax and grammar, spelling, and verb agreement are atrocious but just a breath from her, the smallest utterance and there is no doubt she is tuned in to life not the academy. What she is doing in this classroom of heavy breathers and dislocated minds I have no idea. Her soul belongs to the fields and stables in Northern Virginia where she teaches horseback riding. Her intelligence is born of the sensitivity and shyness of the horses she handles each day. This has freed her to see things as they are, not how humans would like them to be. Like horses she has a quick scent for what is freeing and what is enslaving.

About a French film called *The Red Balloon* she writes, "My favorite aspect of the movie is how the boy (who finds a red balloon and makes a companion of it) always seems to be in his own little world that no one else seems to be aware of, and often gets him in trouble for." Even before she turned in these lines, I sensed someone at the back of the room who did not have that curtain of futile buzzing around them. Her lines were clean, her persona devoid of excess, her demeanor unassuming. While her domain will never be the printed page, I sensed in her the same qualities that drew me to the very best writers.

The boy in *The Red Balloon* could be her, and the horses she saddles each day her red balloon(s). Like the boy, she gave no evidence of any interest in the people around her for the simple reason they have little to offer her. They are the slaves, awaiting the next order, the joyless ones whose souls have flown into some gearbox. She will have a difficult time finding her equal, her other half.

The movie to which she refers, *The Red Balloon*, is a mostly silent one, written and directed by Albert Lamorisse. The "trouble" she mentions comes from the consternation the boy and his balloon cause an entire society. When the balloon follows the boy into his school, the boy is locked by the headmaster in a room in solitary confinement for the day. When he takes it home, his guardian, an old woman, tosses it out. But always the balloon lingers nearby, waiting for its little buddy, the boy. They are tossed off the tram and booted out of church. Outside, in the comparative freedom of the street, they play, tease each other, have a brief flirtation with a little girl who has a blue balloon. The boy and the red balloon carry none of the gravity of the institutions they've been ejected from. On the streets of Paris they grow more buoyant. Their journey becomes a tour of Paris, not the Paris of travel posters but a post-World War II European city whereas the horse-girl notes, "everyone is somber . . . nothing jumps out at all." But the red balloon does. Red is passion, vibrancy, blood and the colorless citizens lighten a bit and permit the red balloon under their umbrellas when it rains and the boy seeks to protect his new playmate.

What more could any of us want out of life than to have a devoted buddy who likes to get outside and fool around? Nothing much happens inside buildings; it is all out in the street – the open air, twists and turns in oddball alleys, a pastry shop for a brief treat, the impending sense of discovery around the next corner. Life, says the red balloon, is about a casual but unending flow with a playmate, about playing, and about the unexpected.

But the unexpected can turn lethal, especially when exposed to the mob. These are the child's schoolmates and when they turn their pent-up wrath on the red balloon, we see the role of all the institutions, including home, who have no room for red balloons; they exist to control the smoldering rage of the mob lest it smash schools, churches, trams, store windows. They direct the bottled and snarling energy of the mob toward someone alone, physically unprotected, vulnerable in its pure affection for life. By their very nature institutions need scapegoats. Scapegoats take the pressure off of institutions and unite the passions of the mob. This is called "society."

The device by which the institution stretches its tentacles and controls the mob is always by virtue of the machine, especially if they can convince the mob that the latest machines are in the best interest of the mob. Thus, a giddy array of cell phones, computers, walkie talkies, etc. give the mob the illusion of control and progress when these devices are just a tightening of the noose around its own neck. As it strangles, its search for scapegoats becomes frenetic. As the horse-girl clearly sees, the modus operandi here is hatred, a denial of all life. As the boys of Paris begin their chase to destroy the red balloon, she writes, "To me this seems like the other boys are trying to destroy the only thing the boy seems to have and care about. I feel like this very act symbolizes so much of how human life is hate."

It is precisely the boy's quiet self-containment and effortless joy the mob resents. With his red balloon he has no need of them. This they resent most of all; they, themselves, have nothing, just the dry, colorless formulas of the school, the church, and the home. Paris then is stagnation and starvation; only the boy and his little balloon, his purity and love of life have any validity.

Audiences in 1957 knew something that the horse-girl was not aware of: periodically the mob slaughters each other on a mass scale. In the 40 preceding years they had done it twice; viruses had gone amuck; speculators had been sent packing. Now, in the year 2009, after a period of glorious speculation around paper money, it is all happening again. And around the world birds, bees, trees, rivers, and red balloons are cheering for the rage of the mob to pick up its pace.

The horse-girl concludes her requiem for a balloon by saying, "After watching this movie I felt happy, almost lighter. I wanted to go for a walk, not do anything that required me to do, well anything. The movie has something that is brilliantly carefree."

The Red Balloon does indeed have something brilliantly carefree. Nothing of the formulaic existence that has dominated the world for the past 25 years can touch it. The red balloon is out there all by itself, teasing and floating on the air waves, waiting for a little partner to come along and enjoy life. People who earn their livelihoods from inside buildings have no idea of its existence. These are massive carcasses filling up with hatred by the hour and eating their way through the crust of the earth right to the center where an inferno is awaiting them.

So, it was the horse-girl and the red balloon who really got me started thinking about all the writers I was indebted to. For it was these writers, in the conglomerate, who reminded me not to take what I was told very seriously, gather up my legs on a Saturday morning and head for the avenues to see what was interesting. I might meet someone who had stories, or someone else who just liked to play; I might meet a cat or a dog who wanted to fool around for an hour; I might just enjoy the sunshine and the fresh air, or spot a different kind of bird wandering into the neighborhood.

If there was a single lesson from those writers, horses, red balloons, enraged boys, and horsey-balloon caretakers, it was this: KEEP THE LEGS IN SHAPE, YOU MAY NEED THEM. Stay agile, stay fleet afoot. Soon there will be no airplanes, buses, autos, trains, or even available horses. If you want to make it beyond the firing range, you have only your feet and legs. And you'd better make a buddy of them before it's too late.

letter from a prague tram

I understand more about that debacle in the Mid-East than any other person on Earth because of an incident on a Prague tram that lasted ten seconds. Fifteen Czechs glared at me with a blazing, calcified hatred I had never seen before and had always associated with individual mad men. Whole nations only went crazy in books, like Elias Canetti's *Auto da Fé*.

My crime? I had woken supremely happy and on the tram sunk into a deep, smiling reverie. I was going to the Charles Bridge (a tourist site) to sell my poetry books; the sun was shining and the air was crisp and I would soon meet my lively friends (all refugees from Bosnia), and hear the gallant Gypsy music from a dozen violins.

Just as important, the day before I had met one of my heroes, Bohumil Hrabal, in a Czech pub, *The Golden Tiger*. When I congratulated this writer on giving his bellhops, waiters, trash collectors formidable innovative powers, he shook his head.

"No," he said, "I am only a link in a wide chain of other writers who showed me the way," and he rattled off a list of writers from six countries including James Joyce.

So, If I smiled it was not with the apparently absurd egotism that started this letter. It was simply that for a few minutes I felt part of creation: the sparkling sunlight, lively air, a few friends who'd escaped from Bosnia with the clothes on their backs, the Vltava River, the wise old man, and the bridge – so monumental in history it has excited several novels. And the wrathful Czechs? The new "capitalism" had merely brought one more invader – ignorant tourists and voracious investors.

When you're happy you know things and I knew immediately what was going on. Luckily for me the next stop was mine and I leaped into a world endlessly flowing through time with silly stories, heartfelt music, and space for the stranger.

The fact is that it doesn't matter whether the U.S. keeps bombing Iraq or quits bombing Iraq; it doesn't matter whether Saddam Hussein stays in Baghdad or shifts his base of operations to Patagonia; the bombing could shift to Toledo, Ohio, and it still wouldn't matter. What's needed is a complete change of heart in all the world because the world's heart is as maimed and calcified as those of that tawdry crew on the Prague tram. Once the heart is open, as we see in small children all the time, anything is possible, even harmony.

I am realistic enough to know that this won't happen until the Earth is invaded by Martians who kidnap Miss Peru only to discover that tattoo on her left buttock that has Zorro decapitating Mickey Mouse won't come out and that ingot in her navel is inedible. After all, wasn't it a snotty, little Austrian named Adolf Schicklgruber – Hitler – who, refused in the rug-cleaning business (he tried to chew them), refused entrance to a Vienna art school (his one topic was droll maidens fainting at the sight of his Charlie Chaplin moustache), understood that a country can only be unified when there's an exterior enemy. The result was 65 million dead, two-thirds of them civilians.

We didn't learn a single thing from wee Schicklgruber except that there are a lot of people in this world who should change their names. But neither had we learned a single thing from the preceding war when an Irishman named Yeats wrote, "The best lack all conviction while the worst are full of passionate intensity." What we did learn from the First World War was that we could market it: "Al Gooey on the Western Front," or "Florence of Arabia" in which Anthony Quinn playing a despondent goat accidentally wanders into Peter O'Toole's tent, and you know the rest. I don't want to be politically or sexually incorrect. I do know we didn't learn anything from the 87 wars in the 19th century except that

Thoreau should have stayed in the woods and Whitman should have left the grocery boys alone; Emily Dickinson's poems should have remained in the desk drawer where they were found when she died; Alexander Herzen should have kept traveling, and Balzac drank too much coffee; Rimbaud, who did more to warn us what was going on than anyone else, was written off as a fizzled prodigy who turned to gun-running out of despair. Each country had and has its voices to remind us there is a way out of polemics and murder, and each voice has been run out of town by that crazed mob on the Prague tram.

So don't listen to me. Don't listen to Hikmet (Turkey) or Buchi Emecheta (Nigeria); don't listen to Albert Cossery (Egypt), Jean Giono (France), or Bessie Head (Cameroon). Don't listen to César Vallejo (Peru), Miguel Asturias (Guatemala), or Dick Gregory (U.S.). Forget what Einstein said or Mozart played, or the words of a few unknowns in rainforests and on mountain sides like Karen Mogensen Fischer. The TV and the newspaper will tell you all you need to know.

But there is one small voice you might want to listen to. It is the voice of a small Iraqi boy whose head wounds are being tended to by a U.S. marine. Not far away is the bullet-riddled car he was riding in where his father is slumped across the driver's seat. His mother, sister, and another relative are having their wounds treated by other marines a few feet away. As the marine is applying disinfectant to the boy's head, the child pulls back and says, "Hey, don't throw any more bombs at us, okay?"

It is not what he says; it's how he says it. There is no plea. No melodrama. He could just as well be admonishing his mother to put peanut butter and not jelly on his toast. "Hey, don't throw any more bombs at us, okay?" It is not important that he is Iraqi nor that he is a child. His voice is that of the Earth, alone of the planets in our galaxy pulsing with blue life. It is a voice that doesn't know the words "guilt", "sin", "flag", "enemy", "success", "our god", "your god", "money", nor "hate".

It's not even important that this child knows the bullets were not "bombs" and may have come from his own people. He simply is offering a voice that says, "I don't want to die; I want to go on living."

Most importantly, there is no blame in this child's voice. He just wants to go on living in the only world he knows, one in which he invents and reinvents, no matter how impoverished his circumstances, sometimes alone, sometimes with his friends, endlessly exercising his imagination and his small muscles. Yes, there is conflict, occasional shoving and a fist fight, but in this child's world revenge is not harbored nor does the heart calcify for the simple reason that it is the pure joy of the game that counts. Movement, something new, and laughter are the code words of the day and within the repetition of certain games, that Iraqi child and his friends will always come up with something refreshing. This is a world very far from the dictates of the priests and the preachers, teachers and politicians, admen and coffin designers, dull fashions and numbing electronic gadgets he will soon encounter.

Every person in the world knows this is true because during vacation times there are few if any fights but when school begins again, the brawls increase. Nobody in any country really wants the education systems as they are now comprised which simply prepare us for the propaganda systems of the priests and politicians and industrialists and generals, and nothing more.

So that Iraqi child's matter-of-fact admonishment is a shriek to the world, "Leave us alone unless you want to sit down and play a new game." Wasn't it Einstein who said, "Truly adventurous spirits always encounter the violent opposition of mediocre minds." At this moment there is not a country in the world which does *anything* right so complete has been the trashing of adventurous spirits. There is no leadership and there will be none. Three years from now we will still be bombing each other and what the bombs don't get, the earthquakes will until millions of children will realize simultaneously that to remain in the company of adults is suicide and they will start running. They will meet in caves and at river beds, at the edge of deserts and in the forests to do what humans have always done: figure out a way to eat, and that done, settle in to some improvised game.

I will be sitting there waiting for them because I am going back to the only group that's ever accepted me – the animals in the rainforest. Yes, I will once again have to shed my large ego, remind myself that I am a *guest* in someone else's creation, and place a little food and water, as I once did before, during the April dry season. My reward? Well, each time I trotted out a portable typewriter to the table on my porch and began to type, a small green lizard took up residence on one of the legs of the table and puffed his throat at the end of each sentence. A dozen Morpho butterflies, each as big as my hand, fluttered into the clearing; and sitting on the tree branch closest to my cabin was Ho Chi Minh, not the warring leader of Vietnam, just a white-faced monkey who looked like him and had been sent by his troops to see what was up with the new vibrations and the strange tourist. When I looked up at him after completing a paragraph, I said to him: "Why do you torment the other monkeys and always take the bananas I give them?" He stroked the white tuft protruding from his chin and looked over the treetops for a long time as if he were searching for an unfathomable answer.

a member of the family: galeano uncorked

Of course I was surprised when a writer whom I considered a member of my personal family was recommended from the president of one country to the president of another a few weeks ago. I didn't know presidents read, or read books that change the chemistry of one's blood. But then I come from a country – the U.S. – where books that rip at the way we think and feel have always been suspect. Even in the institutions of "higher learning", the learned professors don't take Whitman or Thoreau very seriously. "Culture", as relayed by the pundits, was something you poked in after you secured an apartment, a load of groceries, and at least a meeting with a potential mate who was likely to be on the hefty side and after the first kisses demanded to sit on your face. For desperadoes like me, always wandering, constantly probing for some sort of footing that the accepted language could not offer, finding writers whom I could hang on to, refer to again and again when I felt cornered was not easy.

I wanted writers who spoke to some hidden part of me that wanted to rear up and fly with the birds. A lot of writers spoke to this need for an hour or a day like Elias Canetti's *Auto da Fé* or Juan Rulfo's *The Burning Desert*, Nelson Algren's *Man with the Golden Arm* or José Donoso's *The Obscene Bird of Night*. Such books inched me along on my journey but for the most personal reasons, unknown to me, did not become members of my personal family. Eduardo Galeano's work did and I've often wondered why since I have no identification with the downtrodden, the masses, group cooperation, social protest, the lives of dictators, the programs of rebels; words like emancipation, third world, exploitation, imperialist, socialism have no meaning for me. What then of Galeano connected with me on a permanent basis so that I felt the need each year to consult one of his books?

It all begins with a sense of recognition between writer and reader that allows the latter to feel he is traveling with a reliable guide. For example, in *Century of the Wind* Galeano says about Louis Armstrong, "He blows and the music stretches out, out, greeting the day." That's exactly what the best jazz does, it stretches out. From my first love with music, I might even substitute rhythm 'n' blues. It doesn't matter. Someone with a musical instrument has created a separate world that reaches out to touch me, maybe to embrace me, to slide along my nerve endings so that I might feel part of a larger world. It is 1956 and I am in my bedroom looking out on the belching smokestacks of Pittsburgh, Pennsylvania, and listening to The Midnighters sing, "Annie Can't Wok No Moh" and smiling and swaying my hips. I have to go to school but the day is beginning just right. I got me a little juice where I never expected to find it – those Negroes – and they sing so sweetly about something whacky and irreverent – an out-of-work hooker – which no adult will talk about except in derogatory tones but here she is, pacing the floor, 'cause she's pregnant and can't service her men and has to walk the floor, floor, floor. Okay, I'll truck off to school but now that I've had a taste of Annie, I don't have to listen to all the shit they're going to mumble in that silly classroom today.

That's the sort of recognition Galeano could free up and if I am much more verbose than he would ever be, that's okay because true writing isn't about literature, it's about the flights a kindred spirit can induce. It doesn't matter the label you put on these daydreams of recognition, just the fact that you have flown and for a few seconds relieved inertia, broken from jail, and acknowledged the glow of a person who's given shape to his spirit and gotten your little freckled Irish ass moving where before it was content to just sit while the pundits crooned all around it.

I didn't find Galeano till I was in my forties. I don't remember how I came across *Open Veins of Latin America*. In 1987 I met his English translator, Cedric Belfrage, in Cuernavaca, but I think I had read *Open Veins* before that. Belfrage had just finished translating Galeano's trilogy, *Memory of Fire*, and when I found it I didn't read it; I clawed at it, I carried the three books everywhere; sometimes the last volume, *Century of the Wind*, lay next to my pillow. I wanted to greet the day with *Century of the Wind*.

I mention my age because by the time Galeano came along I had read 500 books about exploitation and protest. His work wasn't so much a revelation but a summation. To me it wasn't about how "developed" countries exploit "undeveloped" ones; it was about the air we breath and how it is made up of money and lies. Or lies and money. The two always go together. It was about an attitude found throughout the world, but especially noticeable in the United States, called Fuck or Be Fucked so that sex became business and business was a mechanical form of copulation.

But it wasn't so much what Galeano said, it was how he said it. The very short stories, or prose poems were not a literary form. They were explosions. They were written by a character down to his last resources, his spine arched, a man of the purest molten lava who knew how to touch the brow of a monkey or a woman, a man with the curiosity to make a connection between Saturn and a favela in Rio, between Einstein and a hubcap collector in Mexico City. Here was a man of massive intelligence not writing from his brain but from his liver and his spleen and his kneecaps, in a flash moving through the emptiness in the earth below the former silver town of Guanajuato to a stockbroker's meeting in New York City. Galeano was a reminder of a meeting around 1890 between Baudelaire and a Paris reporter who said to him, "Mr. Baudelaire, you're always complaining about corruption;

exactly what in your opinion is so corrupt?"

Baudelaire just pointed.

"You mean the walls?" queried the reporter.

"No," said Baudelaire, "the wallpaper."

It is my opinion that rage is the fulcrum for Galeano's stories but maybe I feel that because I see him justifying my rage and the notion that words could give it form and I wouldn't spend my life behind bars. I don't think I have ever read. No, I churned along the tortured lining of my intestines and the tepid waters of my brain pan, clawing for a life raft. It was a voice I was looking for, a voice that spoke to me. Because I spent so many years in a vacuum, trying to figure out what the world wanted from me, my own search for this voice distilled and compacted into an explosive form. At age 19, I read Dostoyevsky's *The Idiot* in a single sitting – 23 hours. The real connection between writer and reader is one of temperament and what the schools teach us about books is of no use at all. The relationship happens at that mineral-chemical point of ignition and if superb writers like Galeano teach the reader patience, the reader teaches the writer not to ever give up. If we don't have words – real words fused to the most dynamic flowing language, then we have to reach for a gun, a knife, and when we do that we have forfeited our freedom to explore and to find that occasional miracle that gives us back our breath. The relationship between writer and reader is finally part mystery and part gin. You have to be a little drunk to get along with Galeano (or Asturias, or Henry Miller, or Nikolai Gogol, or make up your own family). They demolish the conventional thinking that gets us our pay checks and playmates. They get us hopping with delight or hopping mad. They set off caresses inside us and sometimes the liver strokes the pancreas and says, "It's going to be alright. There's a few men here speaking the truth." Or they get us so enraged we wish we had gone to bomb school instead of the local university. Then we remember most of our oppressors have gone to Bomb School and that the local university teaches acquiescence to bombers. There has to be a healthier more inventive way of dismantling The Machine and at this point we might reach for Edward Abbey's *The Monkey-Wrench Gang*. Just for starters. Or we go back to a writer who might have been the starting point for Galeano – Euclides da Cunha – his band of beleaguered warriors that exhausted Brazil's military machine 110 years ago.

In one sense Galeano is the culmination of Latin American writing for the past 400 years because he writes with a bluntness that until recently would have got a writer shot or deported. In fact his first 20 years of writing is writing on the run. Galeano writes for all the brilliant Latinos who could not write or wrote elusively in poetry and novels. Still, Asturias and Carpentier have to hide in Europe; Neruda is condemned to death in Chile and flees on a horse. Why don't we know more about the horse? It must have been a hero. Galeano reconstructs the real relationship between Latin America and Europe and the United States and the fact that he sees the world as one may only remind us how ugly our cars are or how treacherous the people closest to us. Wherever we are at we have to tiptoe; the freer we desire to be, the more cautiousness we have to maintain. God on Earth is a snitch and the loneliest of people are the snitches. But Galeano takes it far beyond the rape of the have-nots by the haves. He picks up where Rimbaud left off and patiently shows us invention by invention, hypocrisy by hypocrisy how we constructed a brilliant little Hell in which nobody benefits, least of all the tyrants themselves. He is a constant reminder that nothing works and that we had better change our way fast or the whole earth is going to explode.

For me, it is this urgency of Galeano's that is his ignition point and accounts for those kernels he writes in. He is always on edge because we are a world at the edge of toppling into the black void. It has been this way for a long time but with each Galeano book it gets worse. Yes, there are those saviors he salutes like Neruda, or Bessie Smith, or James Baldwin but even as his vignettes give them back their freshness, we are reminded that nobody has paid much attention to them which is precisely why we are ready to fall down a hole. Sure, there have been valiant warriors all along the way to combat the endless tyrannies, the great mass of inertia keeps building and inching along, not just the materially comfortable with their endless array of electrical toys but the sprawling masses with not enough to eat who are more likely to implode in all directions rather than be herded to a safe corral through reform.

Galeano, whether I read him 25 years ago or yesterday, is a reminder that people don't know how to live and that it is getting late. He takes my personal rage and weaves it among mountains and races so that I see how vast is this Hell I've been dealing with and just how long it has been going on. He reminds me that I am small yet my voice is bigger than all the governments that have ever existed, and that this voice on some days might be nothing more than a handful of seed I put out for the birds. Galeano is a reminder too that almost any sound I hear within civilization on any given day is nothing more than contrived hysteria. It might be the piped in music in a supermarket or two men conversing now behind me on the eternal value of a laptop computer. It might be the memory of some teacher droning on and on 60 years ago or a newscaster 46 years ago advising me that the president of the U.S. has been shot. It is all the same like clumps of cotton candy sticking together at some sad carnival where even the local clown wants to hide his face. It is the year 2009 and the clumps of sticky fiber we have been told won't hurt us are so dominant and so impenetrable, I'm alerted to the fact that fear has won out everywhere and that to try to weave a paragraph that pierces the glutinous mass that engulfs the Earth is, as Ramakrishna would say, like trying to drive a nail into a brick wall.

But not so fast, I tell myself. There is this minor miracle of people hopping on the Galeano bandwagon because some president has handed another president *Open Veins*. Maybe this will set off some reverberations. Maybe somebody will get off their ass and start crippling the machine, or simply say, "I am a guest on Earth," and put out a little bird feed. The possibilities are endless and Galeano has enough individual portraits to remind me it is not society that must change but individuals. God is not a quick-change artist but a blaze of life anywhere we find it. And I don't have to hope for the world; I know how futile that can be. But I can hope for myself and then take the first steps to shed my old skin and grow a new one. Snakes do it all the time, and hell's bells, I'm just as good as any water moccasin. And twice as venomous.

My own urgency here, or Galeano's, shouldn't obscure the fact that he is making stories for us. Good stories, not correctives, are the only things worth having. There is nothing else after food and shelter. But oh to get that food and shelter. For that we have to fake it. We have to cough up some battered words that make the owner of the land bask in the glory of his personal power. When that happens, we begin to shit little pellets instead of the fully blossomed flowers of our personal turds. Is there anyone who doesn't look into the toilet bowl before he flushes? He is looking to see how he is doing. Céline put it best: on this planet we only have two choices, to lie or die. All of the lie is built around the veil draped around the disposal of our waste: body waste, word waste, plastic waste, tree waste. All of it is flushed out to the hole we imagine the sea to kill the fish. Then we eat the fish who have eaten our waste, and having digested, tell our children they must go to school where it is prohibited to talk about certain four-letter words – mostly shit – if you want to be successful like Daddy and Mommy and sit safe and bloated in front of the teevee and fart on cue to the latest commercial. This lemming-like march is circular and perpetual and to meet anyone with the glow of adventure in their eye you have to go to the edge of the earth. If Céline snuck in a bit of the truth, it was because the word-disseminators in Europe knew we were headed for a massive collision. They were right: six years later, September 1st, 1939,

Hitler marched on Poland and in another six years 55 million people were dead, half of the survivors were crackpots, and Céline was in jail. Far from his first two books, he developed his own personal hysteria that made him hang out with the wrong crowd, heap abuse on the wrong crowd.

Writers who sniff the fraud aren't so much individuals as links in the chain who continue Céline's story. Galeano shifts the point of view to a forgotten hemisphere. Animals, trees, mime artists, warriors, villains, and saints come dancing out of the Andes end out of the Amazon River. New recipes, new dances, new masks so as to be able to speak with one's dead relatives.

From the first invention of the 20th century, Galeano will be introduced to Keaton and Chaplin, two waifs who set the tone for his books. The other inventions of the 20th century make sure half the people on earth at any given time are wandering refugees – street waifs in the extreme – all hoping for a miracle to relieve them of the burden of being human and figuring out their role as humans. Of course the miracle is themselves, the miracle of being born; more particularly the miracle of Marcel Marceau whom Galeano salutes and who continues the joy and suffering, absurd comedy and noble tragedy, the continued dance with delicate story line but with a catch: there are no words. Just gestures and the shifting muscles of the face to indicate emotion. Marceau does more without words than all the novelists together in a single year.

Thus, Galeano speaks to me because he speaks to another one of my prejudices: a deep suspicion of words, with an accompanying love of silence. Perhaps this explains the explosiveness of Galeano, the magnificent ignition point of recognition, and the fact that his stories are so short; 200 words is a long story for Galeano. Maybe he doesn't like words, or that our attention span is about as long as it takes to pick a booger out of our nose. The story will be as long as a spark. Hours or weeks later the spark might ignite another story. Or just some daydreaming that will lead to a personal recollection of what is real. He shares with his readership the knowledge that words almost exclusively have been used to cooerce (spelling intentional), cow, and deprave. Like Marcel Marceau he will mostly make the muscles of his face work in their tortured fashion and remind us of what we should have looked at all along. Like Marceau, Galeano is a jerk and a spasm and an occasional caress, all with the facial nerves and muscles. That's where we are at. The days of words are numbered. Our link to the cell phones, computers, and other toys will soon be cut. Then we will wander among the debris and wonder what happened. If we are lucky we will find someone with a fire and some soup and bread. We will help scrape the mold from the bread and have the greatest meal of our lives. Then, only then, the old stories will start again.

the long road to nowhere

Elisabeth Sifton's 5,000-word swansong to the end of book publishing begins, "Humanity has read, hoarded, discarded and demanded books for centuries." Fifty years of bullying by the culture barons has taught me to be suspicious of words like "humanity", "peace-loving", "minor classic". My immediate reaction is that "humanity" hasn't been doing any such thing, Elisabeth. "Humanity" has been busy cooking Uncle Harry by the family gravestone and if they occasionally dabbled in books it was to find a new recipe for ketchup to hide the fact that they were eating human flesh and were really cannibals.

Furthermore, I have good evidence from the leaders of the youth gangs of this United States that Elisabeth herself is going to be cooked soon and eaten. I can only hope that her flesh is more tender and forgiving than it appears to be in this article written for the June 7th, 2009 issue of *The Nation*, one of those darling liberal magazines that are all on the side of freedom as long as threats to it aren't described too bluntly.

First off, most of so-called humanity for the past 150 years doesn't know what the hell a book is. They are herded this way and that, trained to harvest crops, or in times of war kill; like the cattle and sheep they herd, they are butchered when they are ripe. "Progress" is a word used by the politicos, generals, industrialists, and corporations to give the illusion to the masses who have been granted access to language that they are on the right track. The custodians of such words are Sifton and generation after generation of skilled technicians who call themselves "professionals." They are allowed to dillydally and finger-fuck each other in tall office buildings and turn out dainty cultural products as long as they pose no threat to the governing barons. The masses that Dostoyevsky, Cossery, and da Cunha envisioned reading their books have been persuaded it is more profitable to spend their time with electrical toys that go ding and dong and squeak all over the fucking place.

This is called "modernism" or in Spanish "moderna" or "keeping up with the Joneses" and could be anything from a corset laced with molasses to a see-through bra that announces some dolt's readiness to breed. It's not really about anything except that through man's inventions it gets speeded up to the point where people can no longer see or hear. Its result is what we see across the world now: a race of humans so idiotic, so out of tune with themselves and nature that they will soon flush themselves from the planet.

A hint of this collapse in the form of crumbling financial institutions is what prompted Mzzzzz Sifton to write this cautious analysis of her artifact industry. As usual it is written from quite a distance as if this lady editor were positioned at the lens of a telescope and looking out on Saturn instead of her own desktop, which is where the action properly begins on the assessment of a very peripheral industry. The men and women I've met around the earth whom I judged to be healthy, honorable, and content did not read books. Ninety-nine percent of the books ever published were nothing but lies and propaganda, a flexing before the mirror. The handful of writers who went behind the mirror were, like Rimbaud, cursed from the start. They were badgered at every step and eventually hounded into oblivion, poverty, and disgrace even before their own families. Another of them, Jean Giono, is the property of Sifton's employer, Farrar, Straus & Giroux. Yet when I telephoned there ten years ago to find out why Giono couldn't be found in bookstores, I was told he was available through "print on demand", one of those endless euphemisms publishers offer for a writer they no longer want to deal with.

The jargon language that editors, publishers, and agents hide behind is so thick as to constitute a wall. Yet it is no more severe than the smokescreen created by words in a thousand other subspecies known as professionals. They do this to avoid police clubs and to achieve a sense of belonging. Then they pass along this jargon to hundreds of millions of young people in colleges and we are told it is "education". It is no such thing; it is evasive language used to extend the viciousness and cruelty of the people who lay claim to owning the earth. Nothing more. It was like this 400 years ago when the conquistadors were running amuck in the Americas and it has not changed one iota.

Probably Henry Miller has the last word on these professionals when he describes students at a French boarding school who are studying to be professionals: "They belonged to that category of colorless individuals who make up the world of engineers, architects, dentists, pharmacists, teachers, etc. There was nothing to distinguish them from the clods whom they would later wipe their boots on. They were zeros in every sense of the word, ciphers who form the nucleus of a respectable and lamentable citizenry."

Part of the problem is that an elite forms out of the most talented and aggressive of these professionals. In the aftermath of war or economic catastrophe, these elite do adopt new standards – briefly. That is the only way we get the books (or other innovations) of a handful of people who tell the truth like H. Miller, Behrangi, Herzen, Traven, Richard Wright, Hikmet, Vallejo, Asturias, and another 30 or 40 I haven't listed here. This in turn sets off a wave of imitators among the word usherettes and there is a period of 10–15 years of books, newspaper, and magazine articles that lack the gusto and vision of their predecessors. Slowly the old economic machines retool, a minority of the earth fattens, cowardice clogs the arteries of an army of cultural arbiters. Nothing has been learned. Pus accumulates in the word banks; books and articles become deft apologies for hoarding. The money and gun institutions collapse. Chaos and slaughter on the streets. We are at the end of one of those cycles now.

Nowhere in Sifton's long treatise is the word "truth" mentioned. In her world that would be considered arch and heavy-handed. Neither does she talk about the excellence that has been lost over the past 25 years. Excellence is the soft interchange between reader and writer, two people feeling cornered and discovering each other in the privacy of the printed word. This is the intimacy that has been lost in life and the writer is only reminding the reader to restore it. Any worthwhile writer writes with his spine arched and writes from the darkest corner of the street. The professionals who might see such a writer's work into print have no more memory of the street than they have of what they ate for dinner yesterday. It is all spinning around them too fast.

Sifton does acknowledge that some old formulas haven't worked. Well, thank you, darling. What she, and a 100,000 word-bank arbiters, would never acknowledge is just how early in life those formulas get put in place and are impossible to dislodge. The Jesuits have a saying, "Give us a child until he is seven and you can have him after that." Had Sifton stopped for just a second and started poking into these formulas, she would have had to take into account a host of institutions that try to dominate a child's vision of the world. The most prominent of them is the schools. She might even have re-membered a book published in the early '70s that dealt with this, *The Night Is Dark and I am Far from Home* by Jonathon Kozol. No sooner did it hit the shelves than it was banned. At the prodding of Kozol's former students it was reissued ten years later by Simon & Schuster . . . with an apology from the author in the foreword. Now Sifton would have had to talk about just how well oiled the gears of the machine are, how little genuine criticism gets into print, and the entire world of publishing words is just one more club to keep people in line until they reach the slaughter house and their throats are slit.

Any aspirations, any desire to become a real man or a woman, any desire to see words breathe earth and fire and sunlight and hope are crushed before the child is ten years old. Now the child wakes, knowing he is nothing more than a raw carcass to be bought and sold by the highest bidder. That is the legacy Sifton and her crowd support, not freedom, not a love of life during our brief time on this earth.

Sifton and her confederates at Farrar, Straus & Giroux will vehemently claim otherwise, citing their seven Nobel Prize winners and 31 Pulitzer Prize winners. The former was Nobel's apology for inventing dynamite and licensing it to any company that had the money to buy it. The fact that this prize was once given to Maurice Maeterlinck, who stole his prize-winning book from a drug-ridden and impoverished genius in South Africa named Marais, doesn't say a whole lot about its value.

Dozens of scientists and literati protested to the Nobel committee but to this day they have never rescinded the award and Marais died in the gutter and was buried in an unmarked grave.

Don't tell about the value of any aspect of the book industry. I've listened to their amens and apologies for 50 years. They trash anything that is good or honest or pure. And it is not enough that the book industry will soon go the way of the newspaper industry. It is not enough that they will have to take their place in the unemployment line. They once got a hold of words and they thought that was the answer to something. And they fattened on those words with rinky-dink apartments, lots of croissants, and the glow of professionalism all over them. They didn't realize it takes a constant vigilance to make words work. They fell asleep and they got soft, then disdainful that their world was so lightly regarded.

What they don't realize is they are going to be butchered soon. The youth gangs smell the end coming, are hoarding weapons and watching the news. There is absolutely no future for children and grandchildren of anybody. The people who greased the gears of the machine with their respectable phrasing made that possible. Too many people were left out of the feeding frenzy and now they want their pound of flesh. And they will get it. At the first gust of wind of a hurricane, the prediction of a tornado, the first police sick-in because the city can no longer afford to pay them, they will hit the streets with their arsenal. They will explode out of Anacostia or the South Bronx, laughing like kids going to a picnic. And a picnic it will truly be. Noses for appetizers and plenty of blood sausage. No longer will they have to feed on the poor for sustenance; the obese will supply finger-lickin' fingers and the bloated, gobbling carcasses of the respectful citizenry will finally find a use.

It's going to be the best party of the year so bring the aspirin and your favorite gun. And tell your children there was no point at all in having human beings on Earth.

kerouac, the hero we needed

Kerouac is proof that one man, non-affiliated with institutions, can flip a country on its head. I was there. In it and of it. We need Kerouac again, now, fast.

Kerouac is just a small reminder that any human dialogue has to begin without fetters and has to be built around heart or it is sterile. Yes, there has to be intelligence also to give the blood direction but it always begins with heart. Heart wants to explore, play, give of itself. It doesn't ask for a sure bet, or apply a lien before spurting blood; it just wants to expand and glory in its brief life. In a diseased planet such as we have now the singers have all been trashed and the banks and word banks have bought up the avenues and fed the bloodstream with transfusions of fear. It is time to walk away from investment and time to walk out the back door of the schools and time to turn our backs on that mate who would say "be careful" and take our place at the bar and trot out that silly story we've been hiding for years from Mrs. McGillicuddy.

Kerouac's centerpiece *On the Road* features just this kind of spontaneity. Strangers across the U.S. meet in all sorts of places, swap tales, listen to jazz, dance, have romances, read each other their poems, then depart into the night. The Road, if anything, appears circular with any excuse to go anywhere and the destination is not the point but the trip itself. There is terrific attention to the moment delivered with all the casualness of the truly free; there is no hesitation to bring the car to a halt and get out and look at things and marvel at the landscape, particularly as they head into the open spaces of the American West. In Kerouac's *On the Road* everything feels new and glowing and ripe to play with. As Miller once said about Whitman, "It is always 10 a.m. on a Saturday morning in April."

At the same time Kerouac and his buddy Dean Moriarty were exploding across the American frontier, the pundits in the colleges were trotting out T.S. Eliot who advised one and all that "April is the cruellest month". Well, just what was so cruel about it? The pundits at podiums could explain that and we students in 1957 had to repeat this biopsy on civilization so we could get a good grade and our parents would send us more allowance money. The current catastrophe called civilization is nothing more than a lot of people sticking their nose up the ass of some authority figure and calling it progress. Because if you hang tight with T.S. no good can come from wandering down the block and you'd better stay in your dormitory room. Then the pundits can stick more dead snot down your craw and you wake up in the morning calling yourself an "existentialist". Oh my!

Eliot's *The Waste Land* was a closed system with all the weight of European culture on its bank clerk's back. Eliot, like everybody else who was taught, was a pundit's dream. *The Waste Land* depended largely on allusion – all sorts of references to previous culture and historical landmarks – and all us penitents in the front row could do was to scribble frantically and hope the allowance money arrived on time for the next beer bash.

But Kerouac's *On the Road* not only put dynamite to Eliot and all the other drudge that was being offered in the academies, it did something no other book has ever done: it got people in the hundreds of thousands to voluntarily step outside the safety of their homes, and wander across the vast North American continent to discover the nature of the country they had been born in. And they imitated the spirit of *On the Road* by approaching this journey without preconceptions, without prejudice, animated only by the desire to see something interesting and have some stories to tell when they got back home. This alone flies in the face and slams a door on the dozens of bits of bigotry we were taught by our parents, the schools, the media, and conventional wisdom. The "road" was the pathway to freedom that seemed new at the time but was only a reminder of our childhood when we wandered the alleyways of tawdry milltown Pittsburgh, delighting in piles of junk set out for the junkman. In the world of the child, everything is useful; all the world is animated. It was and is that sense of renewal that Kerouac helped us to rediscover.

Luckily, I had read *On the Road* and traveled across the States before I landed in college. Thanks to Kerouac I was able to maintain an aloofness and skepticism toward the bilge that was being offered to me as "higher education."

For me, it all began in that ancient year of 1959. *On the Road* had been out for two years but had just arrived in my Pittsburgh factory town that spring. I first spotted it being passed around in my high school study hall, all battered and taped. Now, nobody but nobody read books where I grew up. It was considered a sign of weakness, akin to playing the violin, or admitting you whacked off to Ava Gardner. It simply wasn't done. Thus, to see my acquaintances and friends, all of them with hefty misdemeanor rap sheets, reading a book could only mean one thing: this unknown tome got seriously involved with "it" – the fervent, delirious copulation we all knew awaited us upon graduation just beyond our sleepy milltown (i.e. Clairton in the movie *The Deer Hunter*). Yet when I asked about the book I was told it was about a trip and that if I were interested I had to put my name on the Sign Up Sheet. The Sign Up Sheet had nine people ahead of me but within a month it arrived one afternoon at my study hall desk. And like the previous readers, I finished *On the Road* within four days. Another Sign Up Sheet was presented to me; this one was for all the people who wanted to go on the road that summer following our graduation. Fifty-three guys had signed up; I was the fifty-fourth. Almost our entire male graduating class. But when it came time to actually hit the road, there were four of us. Someone had talked the other fifty out of the trip.

Thus, *On the Road* acted on us the same way as its hero Dean Moriarty acts on the narrator Sal Paradise, the prototype for Jack Kerouac – the generator that gets people moving. And it had the same galvanizing force on young people all over the States. They took to the open road and discovered on their own what Kerouac had wanted them to see in his book – the massive variety of human beings and the bits of beauty that are everywhere. Just as important, Kerouac, following in the footsteps of Whitman, wanted the reader to get out and see and accept the North American continent as a whole: its people, its rivers, the tawdry and the well-formed, hipsters and beauty queens, mountains, ragged towns, moments of sublime celebration along with bullying, callous cops, sunrises and hangovers, all of it flowing toward the sea in a ragged dance of its own making. The duty of humans then is to accept the miracle of so many odd things moving together, and *get in the flow* – the same thing that Miller says at the end of *Tropic of Cancer*. Not thinking, not analyzing, not culture, not literature. But just this quiet, salient movement down the avenues, out past the towns, across the plains, and following the rivers, toward the source of all life – the sea. As I say, thousands of bored teenagers in 1959, unindoctrinated by the disastrous education systems and disregarding the conventional wisdom of their parents and peers, set out on the road and discovered just this acceptance and sense of the whole, along with their own more gracious movement. After two months on the road, I and my three friends had changed. And we would never be the same.

Fifty years later the migration of young people along Kerouac's route still goes on. Every year I meet young men, often from Sweden or Denmark, in the process of buying a second-hand car, and carrying a copy of *On the Road*. Curiously, it's not something they want to talk about . . . till later that night after they have swilled two quarts of beer. Then they become a veritable fountain of diarrhea with their hopes for the road and their utter disdain of the grasping, hoarding bourgeois values Stockholm and Copenhagen have taught them. And this in turn raises the dark underside of Kerouac and company's joy rides for salvation – the reliance on greater and greater quantities of booze, pot, and amphetamines to get that buzz to make a pathway through the mounds of inertia that is everywhere at all times. When does a lubricant for exploration turn the imbiber into a soggy mass of disjointed blubbering? At what point did a great artist like Kerouac become a useless martyr?

But there is nothing disjointed about *On the Road*. In its announcement that there were surprises and exuberance to be found on the road, it wasn't so much a book as a summons to our deepest spiritual reserves. We stuck out our thumbs, or climbed in an old jalopy, or swung into a moving freight train as if reporting for active duty, but not in an army of mechanistic conquest, but a volunteer army fully prepared to grow new eyes, to listen patiently wherever it was required, to set aside our judgments and listen to the species tell its stories. And oh were there stories! Because the United States is historically the loneliest of all countries, anybody and everybody had their life story to tell us. There were moments of humor and insight but mostly they were sad stories ("sad" being one of Kerouac's favorite words) about dislocation, separation, and loss. At the time I was 16 or 17 years old, listening to grown men's confessions, their ribald and exaggerated tales of their sexual prowess, their heartbreak at not seeing their kids for months at a time under a judge's restraining order (the War Between the Sexes was in high gear even in those years). Of course this would only last a month or two before we slipped back into civilization to sip at the well of bourgeois hoarding. Like Sal Paradise when he splits in a very sad way from the tiny Mexican girl with a child and deserts his one true love because he can't hold down a job, we too had to desert The Road because we had no skills and no money. But in those cross-country trips between 1959 and 1968, all initiated by Kerouac, I found my true university and the beginnings of the antidotes to the verbal rubbish that would be shoved at me for the next fifty years.

What *On the Road* offered me and thousands of others was a host of necessary virtues we had lost ten years earlier as we were incorporated into The Mob:

> curiosity
> faith that we would be treated well by strangers
> wonder
> awe
> belief in our own capacity to navigate in strange territory
> total belief in the present moment
> ability at a glance to take in the world as a whole
> the notion that everything was animated.

In other words, the world of The Child. Each chunk of road and accompanying vehicle has its demands which we, and Kerouac and cronies, learn as we move. Because everything is new we adapt quickly to those demands. Such duties were as old as the first group of humans in a cave. If you didn't have a song to sing, that was fine, but you better damn well listen. And if you didn't have a story to tell, that was fine too, but you'd better have the patience to listen to a story. If you were hitchhiking, you'd better have a driver's license and the ability to steer a car safely cross country.

This innocence, openness, and enthusiasm are the foundation of Kerouac's *On the Road*. All nuances and movement spring from them. It is a book of exploration, not a novel of manners. If *On the Road* has any connection with what is known as "literature" it is with *Huckleberry Finn* and Whitman's *Leaves of Grass*; it heeds the command of Horace Greeley fifty years earlier to "Go West, young man, go West." It has no connection with the heavyweight culture of Europe but unwittingly it has all sorts of connections with U.S. Indian folklore, especially the Plains' Indian tales of the Winnebago Trickster. In its love of freedom and physical movement it is purely American. As Miller once noted, "Europe has yet to produce a truly free man." Perhaps this is what accounts for Europe's fascination with Kerouac and black America's jazz art. In the early 1960s, when rock 'n' roll was pushing jazz musicians out of the clubs, they could always find a new home in Stockholm, Paris, or Copenhagen. Kerouac today has more meaning for Europeans than he does for the young in his own country.

If this last paragraph seems a bit egotistic, born out of a single U.S.er's xenophobia, consider the journals of the Russian Alexander Herzen (1812–1870). Rare, he said, was a gathering of Europe's intellectuals, revolutionaries, utopians that the word "America" did not come up in the conversation. Throughout the 19th century as kings and queens were deposed and city-states formed into nations, all of Europe looked to North America as the place where humans could start afresh, free from all the bitterness accumulated through centuries of war in Europe, where there was enough to eat and the average workman could wake in the morning with a reasonable hope that he would be treated fairly that day. The industrial revolution had bred along with work for the masses, over-crowding in the cities, overpopulation everywhere. Europe was simply too small and too divisive, hence the two world wars that opened the 20th century. In the meantime Europe was sprouting ideologues and artists by the bucketful on every corner, all of whom were warning the reader of the coming debacle. Perhaps because they were so far away from the States they had a tendency to romanticize it in Paul Bunyan proportions. But those Europeans who actually visited the U.S. in the 1800s saw something else. "There is a great dream here," said Chesterton, "but I fear it runs aslant." De Tocqueville was even more precise; he foresaw the material demands of a huge mob overwhelming all other considerations.

Herzen, without the benefit of actually visiting the U.S., took Chesterton's "aslant" and hammered away: "Society (American), the majority, seized the powers of a dictator and of the police; the people themselves fulfilled the function of Nicholas Pavolich (Czar of Russia), of the Third Division and of the executioner; the people, who eighty years ago proclaimed the "Rights of Man", is disintegrating because of the "right to flog." Persecution and victimization in the Southern States (which have set the word *Slavery* in their flag, as Nicholas once set the word *Autocracy* in his) in the form of their thought and speech are not inferior in vileness to what was done by the King of Naples and the Emperor at Vienna.

"In the Northern States 'slavery' has not been elevated into a religious dogma; but what can be the standard of education and freedom of conscience in a country which throws aside its account-book only to devote itself to tables that turn and spirits that knock – a country which has kept in being all the intolerance of the Puritans and Quakers!

"In milder forms we come across the same thing in England and Sweden. The freer a country is from government interference, the more fully recognized its right to speak, to independence of conscience, the more intolerant grows the mob; public opinion becomes a torture chamber; your neighbor, your butcher, your tailor, family, club, parish, keep you under supervision and perform the duties of a policeman. Can only a people which is incapable of inner freedom achieve liberal institutions?"

If I have quoted at great length a warrior 100 years and 3,000 miles removed from Kerouac's terrain and time, it is because Kerouac in *On the Road* dealt with every one of the above themes to the point that he challenged everyone to live their lives instead of drifting with conventional wisdom (the voice of the mob) in a hopeless sputtering of demented inertia. That he wasn't recognized for the Great Voice to Wake the Sleepers is just further proof for all that Herzen says in the preceding paragraphs.

To be sure, at the same time Herzen was performing his eulogy on the United States, Walt Whitman was composing his *Leaves of Grass* that was to have such an influence on Thomas Wolfe and his *Look, Homeward Angel*. Wolfe with all of his melancholy yearning was the most dominant influence on Kerouac and melancholy is as pronounced in *On the Road* as is the child-like innocence to combat it. What Whitman argued for in his poems and essays (later collected under *Democratic Vistas*) was the "New Democratic Man." *Leaves of Grass* relentlessly catalogues such men in the form of farmers, lumberjacks, blacksmiths, wagon repairers, horse trainers, fruit-pickers, etc. In other words, workers and craftsmen, and more importantly adults who worked mostly in the outdoors and whose labors depended on their skill and their endurance and not on their ability to insert their noses in the crack of some foreman's rectum. Whitman speaks eloquently of the glint of freedom in their eyes, their broad shoulders, and their overall physical robustness. In other words, the new, free man, free of European oppression, who, according to Whitman, would eventually change the world's definition of what was a man, what was a true woman. Plenty of land, plenty of freedom, and Whitman has them all marching West (presumably under the Homestead Act) to tame a small piece of the wilderness to wrest their livelihood from nature while never taking too much and honoring the rivers and the forests with an intuitive conservation that would make the fields and the water supplies endlessly renewable.

If Whitman's valuable but Pollyanna vision seems a bit much under our modern-day cynicism, keep in mind Kerouac heavily subscribed to it. Contrary to the image of the press and his supposed role as "the leader of the Beatniks", Kerouac thought the United States quite a terrific place; it had given his French-speaking ancestors a chance to revive their lives and live in a modicum of peace and prosperity. To the horror of liberals, Kerouac announced on television that the United States belonged in Vietnam. Everything he said in front of reporters damaged book sales and after the PR folks at Viking pulled him aside for a little chat, he clammed up in front of the press, giving vague one-word answers to baby scribes who were expecting a live, hepped-up version of the maniacal Dean Moriarty and instead got a writer who could have been press secretary to George Bush, father or son. It was marvelous comedy: the press didn't know what to make of Kerouac, except that he was the head of some sort of restless youth movement, supposedly akin to "Hemingway's Lost Generation"; Kerouac, in turn, was baffled at the public reaction to *On the Road* and retreated to his typewriter in his mother's house, typing away for the pure fun of typing. His liver exploded when he was 47.

It should be noted here that when the great writers step down from their art to address the masses on political or religious issues, they invariably make a mess of it. Kerouac wasn't the first. Knut Hamsun and Ferdinand Céline with their political announcements and affiliations created an absolute mess for themselves which to this day discourages liberal-minded folk from reading them.

Not in press interviews, but in his art, Kerouac feels that the only way to approach the vast northern part of the continent called The United States of America is to try to see it as a whole and forget all the divisive splinters that stick in the hands and feet and reduce the aspiring creator to quarrelsomeness. Not in reform but in acceptance *On the Road* implicitly cries out on every page. In spiritual terms it is what might be called a leap of faith. It seems like a leap to the Moon, given the havoc people create for each other, but Kerouac had for a tool and for inspiration an even bigger leap of faith than his efforts at constantly restructuring *On the Road* – the Blues and Jazz from the most downtrodden group in history, blacks who offered the one art form from the U.S. that's respected around the world.

The saga of the Birth of Blues and its grandson Jazz, in all its forms, is one of the great stories of a race bouncing back from the edge of spiritual extinction to remind two-thirds of the Earth just what it is to be truly alive. Jazz may have begun as an offspin of funeral wakes in New Orleans in 1900 but by 1960 when Louis Armstrong toured Africa, and was followed everywhere by tens of thousands of tribal members with their cattle in tow, jazz had come full circle. It was not merely The Music that regalvanized the world but from 1925 to 1960 was something approaching religion. In 1968 I could go into any bar or cafe in the West End of London and hear jazz; the same held true with Amsterdam and Geneva in 1969. It was swing jazz that relieved U.S.ers of their tedium in the 1920s and that decade labeled The Roaring Twenties wouldn't have roared without Duke Ellington and Louis Armstrong. White America finally found something to do with its collective ass – swing it.

Yet I, for one, did not see the miracle of the Blues until I read the history of African blacks being stashed on slave ships and sold at auction throughout the Americas. At the same time I was reading how slavery was the foundation of every major civilization throughout history including the great empires of Latin America – the Olmecs, Aztecs, and Incas. Again Herzen:

"A conquering tribe naturally enslaved the conquered, and on its slavery founded its own leisure, that is its development. Properly speaking, it was by means of slavery that there began the State, education, human liberty. The instinct of self-preservation led to ferocious laws, and unbridled fantasy completed the rest. Tradition, handed on from generation to generation, wrapped the origins (of slavery) more and more in a rosy cloud, and the oppressive, just like the oppressed slave, bowed in terror before the decalogue, and believed that it had been dictated by Jehovah on Sinai to the flash of lightning and crash of thunder, or instilled into an elect man by some parasitical spirit dwelling in his brain. . . . The forms and scenery alter but the principles are the same."

In other words, Kerouac inherited what we all inherit – an atmosphere saturated with slavery and fear and an absolute fear of freedom. This by itself explains a human's propensity for groups and a desperation for group-belonging as opposed to moving quietly across the earth and thinking things out for himself. It goes a long way toward explaining Kerouac's need to go it alone and the massive resistance to *On the Road*.

But as I say, he had allies – this mountain of brilliant black music. Each of the four sections of *On the Road* culminates in a jazz scene and does so with such intensity and virtuosity that there can be no doubt that music is the foundation with which he spent so much time building his book. So jazz forms not only the inspiration for Kerouac but becomes as well his method of construction. Because he inherits no language to recapitulate jazz's vast terrain, he must invent one and this accounts for the freshness and spontaneity of *On the Road*. Fifty-three years later it reads even better than it did when it was first published. Each paragraph is organized along the principle of a series of jazz chords with the principal characters – Cassady, Ginsberg, Burroughs, and others who receive their solo time wail mightily and brilliantly in the tradition of bebop but don't always make sense . . . till the reader reviews their rants in the context of the entire novel.

This bebop, and I would assert here a host of other jazz forms – swing, cool jazz such as the version of "Autumn Leaves" with Cannonball Adderley and Miles Davis – is Kerouac's answer to the slavery (Moriarty would call it "hung up") he finds about himself at all times. In this he echoes Miller's contention that it is not liberal reforms that will wake up the world but emulation of the values of the artist who Miller says is the only one who can heal contradictions. In 1957 when the book was released, none of the reviewers picked up on this. In a "civilized" world where fashion dominates intellectual products just as much as it does the cut of the hem of a woman's skirt, anything genuinely fresh and revitalizing is going to baffle the pundits. In the spring of

2007, National Public Radio in Washington, D.C. convened a panel of experts to celebrate "Walt Whitman Day"; poems of old Walt's were read; the pundits summarized his life and his contributions as one among a handful of writers who were the foundation of American literature. Their conclusion? The United States wasn't yet "ready" for the writings of Walt Whitman. In other words, because of mounting intolerance, lack of openness, resistance to poetic forms, U.S. society, though 70% had gone to college, had taken several steps backward. Advanced schooling hadn't done them any good at all; it had in fact made them more stupid.

The same month I was teaching a course called "African-American Literature" at a southern Virginia college called James Madison. As I was instituting a jazz component in the course, I asked my 40 students who was John Coltrane? Twenty of them were blacks, between 19 and 23 years old; twenty were whites of the same age. After two minutes, a white girl at the back of the room raised her hand. After class, the same girl came up to me and expressed shock that none of the blacks knew perhaps the greatest of the jazz saxophonists from the 1950s. But how many whites know what Jack Kerouac and his hero Dean Moriarty really stand for? Or for that matter The Beatles, Nina Simone, or Wolfgang Amadeus Mozart? Charles Drew, Albert Einstein, or Bessie Smith? The list could go on and on. Humans of all races never lacked for geniuses but if this is so why are humans in such a deep hole now with no way out? Is it simply because they have mislabeled them and not understood their achievements, their way out of divisiveness, slavery, and misery; or simply forgotten them altogether? Of one thing I am certain, humans at this moment in history are totally lost.

The case of Kerouac and *On the Road* is however unique because he understood that the young of America had gotten no instruction whatsoever. He would correct that. He would give them a whole new mythology on how to live. There are hints throughout *On the Road* that Kerouac was interested in a great deal more than relaying some picaresque adventures of a rebellious youth or erecting a hymnal to some disenchanted group called "Beats". On page 231 of the British Penguin paperback edition he says, "The bottom of the world is gold and the world is upside down." This is typical of much of the writing – arcane, mysterious, poetic, jazzy, and seemingly out of context – till you realize this is exactly what Kerouac wanted to do – flip the world on its head, and without bothering about the perversity of those who run the show, reveal the joy, the vitality, the truthfulness of the underbelly of America. All those considered eccentric, castoffs, rum-dums, losers, malcontents, vagrants, tramps, bums, hobos, drunks, whores, poets, dope addicts, sullen Indians, dumfounded blacks, would all be lifted to the surface for the true generosity and hopefulness that is missing from the established order. Corporate managers, government legislators, university intellectuals, department store owners, successful novelists – the overseers and lubricants of the petite bourgeoisie tyranny – simply don't exist, are not worthwhile talking about. As all mythologists have done, Kerouac is creating a new hierarchy – not of human importance – but of values. The society of Kerouac is communal; it's the party that counts not the possessions; spontaneity will replace calculation; celebration will overtake hoarding. And surrounding it all will be that delirious, improvised bebop jazz.

To be sure, beginning with Whitman, the U.S. has a long line of writers, most from the Midwest, defending the oppressed and the outraged: Stephen Crane, Theodore Dreiser, Jack Conroy, Nelson Algren, Studs Terkel, John Steinbeck, and dozens of others writing from a populist sympathy. What separates Kerouac from the pack is his creation of a genuine hero, Dean Moriarty, whose explosiveness and ultimate understanding sails far beyond the boundaries of accepted rationality. In other words, a religious hero.

As recently as 1991, the dominant spokesman in our era for Mythology, Joseph Campbell, announced from his pulpit at

Sarah Lawrence College, that the chronic breakdown in every area of U.S. society could be blamed on the lack of a working mythology. But I have to take it a step farther. What young people didn't have in 1955 and don't have now are people they can look up to for guidance, heroes and heroines. For the last 15 years I've asked my students at numerous universities around the U.S. if they had a hero. Ninty-nine percent shook their heads. There was one young man however who raised his hand. He was from Kenya and had been in the U.S. for eight years.

"Who is your hero?" I asked.

"My brother."

"Your brother! What makes your brother so special?"

"He was a salesman and he can talk just about anybody into buying anything."

Without real heroes who see the whole point of being on Earth, young people are going to be taught two things: How to lie and How to steal. And that's what has been going on for the past 200 years in Western Society, a lot of bullshit and a lot of Thievery. And nothing more. As any 15-year-old could have told you in 1955, all this talk about Progress is nothing more than an attempt by adults to put a rope around his neck. Or, as Henry Miller noted, "The logic of Western society is little more than a hangman's logic."

This is more than some maverick's assertion; between 1939 and August of 1945, 55 million people were killed in a war that originated in the capitals of the supposedly most advanced race of civilization. As a member of first the U.S. Navy, then the Merchant Marine, Kerouac knew all about this meaningless destruction which accomplished the same as the First World War – it made the world safe for investment. That's why, other than jazz and W.C. Fields, there are no cultural references in *On the Road*. A Europe that is in rubble shouldn't have much to say about the value of Shakespeare, Diderot, Plato, Aristotle, John Stuart Mill, Voltaire, Goethe, Molière, Tolstoy, Ibsen, Kafka, etc., etc. What good is culture when it can't avoid wholesale destruction? The very word prompted Henry Miller to entitle one of his essays, "When I Hear the Word Culture I Reach for My Revolver."

Thus, Kerouac can truly begin on a blank page.

He will construct a new world out of just what comes to his senses. But this exhilarating freedom has a huge price; the earliest versions of *On the Road* are a bubble of restless ferment and as someone on the Internet recently pointed out, the final version of *On the Road* is as much a result of a Viking copy editor's rewriting as the rewrites that Kerouac himself did. The real version, that which Kerouac would have wished, we will probably never know, but what we have is plenty.

From the first page when we get news of Dean through some letters sent to a friend from reform school, we know we are on the right track. Moriarty at twenty has a felony rap sheet that would have been the envy of Charles Dillinger. He was the errant waif on the block every mother in America in 1955 warned their wavering son about: "It's not what you know but who you know that counts in this world," they banalized in kitchens across the U.S. It was an admittance that nepotism, incompetence, and corruption ruled the world and there was nothing to do but stick your nose up the rectum of the next bully on the block.

The Mothers of the Earth hadn't learned a fucking thing from World War II though it was their sons that were butchered, their daughters who were bombed. Let's not hear a single further word about Women's Liberation; both genders are educated by the same insane forces, and neither gender has learned a thing except to beat on the opposite sex when they get bored with their mundane jobs. Haul down Liberation from banners everywhere because the only freedom people have learned is the freedom to annoy their neighbor by yapping in a cell phone at five times the normal volume as when they talk to a person next to them.

No, in 1955, every block in America had a version of Dean Moriarty and us punks flocked to him because he was the ornery street waif who got into trouble at every turn, could be seen everywhere at all hours, and had none of the fear or authority we had been taught to have. As Miller said in one of his early books, our first heroes grow out of our playmates on the street. From them we learn to explore the unknown, lose our fear of strangers, develop the nimbleness of our fingers (at theft) and additional speed in our legs (running from the cops). Moriarty was more. He hungers for any playmate he can learn from and has a zest for life, as the narrator Sal notes, that can only be found in those who have been jailed for a long period of time.

Moriarty is the lowest of the low in U.S. society, on his own since he was four, sleeping in doorways at night, pleading before judges in the daytime for the release from jail of his father. Accepted by no one, fitting in nowhere, perpetually on the road, marked for a life of incarceration by the age of ten. None of what we call "civilization" has touched him. Along the trail of Western literature, he is one of Dostoyevsky's damned like *The Idiot*, Knut Hamsun's young narrator in *Hunger*, Jean Giono's circus acrobat, Bobbi, in *The Joy of Man's Desiring*. Like Céline's Ferdinand in *Journey to the End of the Night*, they are outcasts whose first mature thought is that they probably shouldn't have been born. But unlike Ferdinand, the other mentioned outcasts here are catalysts for change. As Herzen would say, they are the people who wake the "sleepers." Deprived of access to even a life of menial labor in people's organization, these are the eternal outsiders. They not only see the sham of civilization, a handful of them invent entirely new systems: Jesus Christ, Ramakrishna, Mohammed, Mahatma Gandhi, Buddha, Helen Keller, Karl Marx, Charles Darwin, Sigmund Freud. Marx saw in his lifetime what Christ might have seen had he lived a little longer: his followers were going to fuck up everything. "Please don't call me a Marxist," Marx pleaded. Darwin had nothing to do with the statement "survival of the fittest," Gandhi insisted that millions of craftsmen would save India but ten years after his death those craftsman were selling plastic flower pots imported from America. Helen Keller tried to launch a worldwide crusade on behalf of all workers but is mainly associated with overcoming personal disabilities. Freud saw the limitations of his analyses among the neurotic of the wealthy and middle class and wanted nothing to do with his disciples. Like Dean Moriarty, Christ, Bobbi, The Idiot, and Mohammed are generally at a loss for words; they teach by example. The few words they offer up are not of knowing but of gladness. Their spirit and their lives are a massive illustration of the futility of words. They know words are but a smokescreen so the butchers can impose their will and enslave the multitudes. Or, the multitudes can enslave everyone by carefully separating word from deed in order to complete separation and ensure a few comforts. Jane Goodall, the chimpanzee woman, writing from the forests of Gombe in Africa, understands fully the limitation of words:

"It is all but impossible to describe the new awareness that comes when words are abandoned. One is transported back to the world of early childhood when everything is fresh and so much of it is wonderful. Words can enhance experience, but they can also take so much away. We see an insect and at once abstract certain characteristics and classify it – a fly. And in that very cognitive exercise, the wonder is gone. Once we have labeled the things around us we do not bother to look at them so carefully. Words are part of our rational selves and to abandon them for a while is to give free reign to our intuitive selves."

Goodall's perfect truthfulness here underlines the difficulty Kerouac had in making *On the Road*. How do you create a coherent book for Western readers when your hero is little more than a ball of tawdry, fervent chaos when Sal, the narrator, first meets him? While Moriarty becomes a great deal more than that by the end of the book, how, as a writer, do you advance a narrative structure when the major vehicles of your word movement are emotions the reader has long forgotten: wonder, wholeness of vision, keenness of hearing, awe, joy, a desire for kindred spirits, animation of all of life, total absorption in the present moment, curiosity, openness to the stranger and the strange? Because it is a world without ego, it has all the energy of original creation. And . . . one of its major fears. Which I'll get to in a moment.

For the task Kerouac set himself there is no vocabulary. Certainly since the Industrial Revolution, humanity has been so busy being busy – the supreme virtue of the new bourgeoisie – lost among the banal and the hopelessly trivial that it has lost the main ingredients of the introduction to life. As the circus entrepreneur P.T. Barnum noted around 1905, "Nobody ever lost money in overestimating the gullibility of the American people." But his remark is not limited to the United States. Gárcia Marquez, in a story entitled "A Very Old Man with Enormous Wings", has delicious fun with a small town in northern Colombia and its persistent gullibility at being seduced by the latest fad of a traveling circus. Anywhere today, people are just as afraid of happiness as they are of failure. This is why they periodically trot out all their prejudices and bomb each other's civilizations into rubble, announce victory, and start the whole dreary process all over again. H. Miller, always the sage, advises us to root on such destruction, as it's inevitable anyway.

Kerouac solved the problem by avoiding a linear narrative; instead he would make each paragraph a prose poem, a complete entity in itself; past, future, and present would be flipped around in short spaces till Time itself dissolved. All sorts of non sequiturs would be fired at the reader in a single paragraph, conversations mixed with glimpses of landscapes out the window, he would jump around freely, always building on a handful of emotions. Each of the four trips would build on the emotions of the previous trip. For his other major organizing principles he would have jazz – fleshed out in further detail with each trip – and the growing stature of Dean Moriarty, his progress from generating balls of chaotic fire to understanding spokesman for what is most needed to feel alive. Contrary to what Kerouac himself said about his banging out the entire book in three weeks in 1951, it took up to 1957 and endless rewrites. And he had the help of Malcolm Cowley, senior editor at Viking Press.

Without Cowley, Kerouac doesn't exist. Cowley is to Kerouac what John Martin was to Bukowski, Barney Rosset was to Henry Miller, Max Perkins was to Hemingway, Vissarion Belinsky was to Gogol. He has Kerouac telescope the many trips into four so as to avoid repetition. He sends Kerouac back to the typewriter to clarify dozens of items. He is so respected in the comparatively tiny publishing and reviewing industry that merely knowing that Cowley is associated with a given manuscript is enough to get it reviewed in hundreds of magazines and newspapers across the U.S. Not that anybody understood it but in the late '50s *On the Road* was talked about everywhere, though the schools and colleges were careful not to mention it for the next 25 years till finally it got lumped under a course for "Beat Literature" at the more progressive places. It was Cowley who in this period published an essay decrying the fact that most of William Faulkner's work was out of print. Faulkner's novels and stories got back into print, in a hurry; a few years later he won the Nobel Prize though Cowley did not have the luck with him that he had with Kerouac of getting him to insert a period once in a while.

On the Road has been labeled a rebellion against the prevailing middle class mores of post-war United States; nothing could be farther from the truth. If there is rebellion against bourgeois values in *On the Road* it is 98% implicit. The five instances in the book of explicit attack against the status quo are all very brief. No, Kerouac wasn't interested in attacking the corruption or inertia of white civilization because he had a far more important issue at stake – Fear of the Night. All of Sal's sense of fragility and vulnerability, his despair and his melancholy happen at dusk or in the night. Toward the end of his first trip, he says:

> "That night in Harrisburg I had to sleep in the railroad station on a bench; at dawn the station masters threw me out. Isn't it true that you start your life as a sweet child believing in everything under your father's roof? Then comes the day of the Laodiceans, when you know you are wretched and poor and miserable and blind and naked, and with the visage of a gruesome grieving ghost you go shuttering through nightmare life. I stumbled haggardly out of the station; I had no more control. All I could see of the morning was a whiteness like the whiteness of a tomb. I was starving to death."

Whether any of us have ever had to wander city streets at night, from bench to bench, doorway to doorway, wandering in icy winds, half-frozen and desperate, not knowing who or what to turn to, not knowing who will pounce on us, the police or a group of beggars, as in this book Miller, Stettner, Bukowski, and Traven have done, and I would add Bessie Smith, Billie Holiday, Gordon Parks, and at any given time a fifth of the world's children (just look at the statistics for Rio de Janeiro, Brazil), Kerouac in this haunting passage, and a dozen more similar ones, is responding to mankind's oldest fear – Fear of the Night. It is fear of the night that accounts for the cave paintings at Lascaux in France. It is fear of the night and that we might not have a place in the world, a shelter to protect us, just a little food before we lie down at night, the warmth and sympathy of some familiar face we can turn to when the demons tear at our sleep and we are reminded how mentally and physically inept we are, and how eventually bombs, or animals, or disease are going to rip out or rot our guts anyway. The night is always a reminder of our aloneness and how brief our stay is on this earth. Fear of the night is our goad to take our place among the living creatures of the earth and find our true calling and above all find a way to celebrate the gift of life, our own vitality and everyone else's. That is why we must search for our voice – to encircle the demons of the unknown and disarm them. The night is why we look for love, why men spend years in dark caves painting figures of beauty, why adults until 1975 on the islands of Malaysia woke their children when they heard them scream out in the night; what exactly did you see and hear?; they took this information to the village and actors, mask-makers, painters, and singers immediately went to work; the next morning the child with the haunting nightmare was presented with his demons by the local artisans, only demons ridiculed, demons disarmed, a hero presented, and a lot of color, song, and plain beauty to remember for a lifetime. The nightmare as theater, horrors transformed, life livable again. Kerouac wants nothing more.

If you want an idea of the horror of the night and the miracle of the sun, follow me to the rainforest of the Nicoya Peninsula in Costa Rica where I lived for five months in 1993. Each morning at 5:45 a.m., all the creatures in the trees – howler monkeys and capuchin monkeys, pumas, and coatimundis, 70 species of birds, anteaters, numerous other mammals, would in unison roar their approval when the sun inched out of the sea. This roar lasted 30 to 45 seconds and it was so loud it could have deafened any crowd in a European soccer stadium. Not knowing anything of cause and effect, the animals and insects greet the arrival of the sun as a miracle. Their roar is their song – their attempt at jazz – to give thanks for one more day of life. Though 90% of them – the monkeys excepted – do their foraging for food at night, night is still a time of terror for them. For the monkeys, dusk is a time of great quarreling because not one of them wants to have to sleep near the main trunk of a tree since that makes them most likely to be snatched away and eaten by a puma. Humans, like other primates, do not have the keenness of eye or ear or the physical agility to compete for food in the night with other species.

Picasso (who stole most of the ideas for his art from Africans) said it all: art has only one purpose – to disarm the terror of the night. Now we see why Sal often grows melancholy, especially when he's alone, at the approach of night. We also see why Moriarty makes disjointed philosophical pronouncements like, "And then we'll all be off to sweet life, 'cause now is the time and we all know *time*." (Italics Kerouac's.) Moriarty knows all about "time" because he's been previously abandoned to the night and is overcoming his fear by trying to grab hold of life as fast as he can. He doesn't have time for words; he must drive as fast as he can, eat fast, listen fast to jazz, sweat all the time because throughout *On the Road* he is nearly terrified that he will lose his hold on life and the night and his sense of abandonment will take over. His one consolation is his kindred friendship with Sal, the narrator, whom he abandons in Mexico because he is so driven (he must get back to an old girlfriend) he loses track of any code. He is a very flawed hero but one necessary in the Kerouac vision. He's a start, a tear in the curtain of massive inertia that substitutes trinkets in place of real vision to overcome darkness.

The legacy of the night throughout human history has one other component, a leader who can show the tribe the path out of darkness. This leader is variously called "seer", "visionary", "dreamer", "shaman", "poet", "medicine man", "healer" and his ritual chants are just as important as his knowledge of healing plants and dangerous berries. Indeed, it is only in the white man's world that the word "poet" has a negative connotation. In what is known as "The Third World" it still stands for wisdom and leadership, at least for those over 40. For it is such a figure who will see the big picture, the past and the future, and help the tribe navigate and not get lost in its day-to-day survival. To this day, the Yaqui tribe in Northern Mexico sends its most promising poets to the desert to partake in the annual peyote rites. With the aid of this hallucinogen, they will be able to compose (in their heads) more encompassing and more profound poems celebrating the white-tailed deer which is the centerpiece (like the buffalo once was for the

Plains Indians of North America) of the Yaquis. Hallucinogens, and stimulants, are regularly used but only a few times a year, under strict controls, and only with select members of the tribe. Whether they are desert or rainforest tribes, their survival is too problematic to permit the self-indulgence of booze and pot that we see everyday and in *On the Road*.

These "seers", wakers of the sleeping, correctors of the past, alerters to what is worth keeping, emerge in the strangest ways, often through the most dangerous initiations. Every country and every region has a great store of lore and mythology about them. Kerouac's antecedents are not in modern literature but in the tales of the Winnebago Trickster from the Plains Indians such as the Sioux. Such a future leader begins under the most unpromising of circumstances; he is branded an undesirable and, booted out of the tribe; as a youngster he is too unruly, too mocking of his elders, too discouraging to daily survival. He is also sexually endowed with oversize gonads (see Márquez's *Autumn of the Patriarch*) and a prodigious dong; in this he is a threat to the other males of the tribe. He wanders by himself in the wilderness (his initiation, which parallels the "walkabout" of the aborigines of Australia) for a long period of time. Imbued with all the guile of nature, he eventually returns to the tribe. But not as a man. Here the cautionary part of the tale enters because in Sioux interpretation the castoff slinks around the village in the form of a coyote. It is man's way of saying, "Be careful what you kill in nature; it may be the force that finally liberates you." When the men of the tribe go off on the hunt (or in Moriarty's case to their jobs in office buildings) the coyote sidles up to the tent flaps, sneaks inside, changes back into a man, and seduces all the women in the village. In some Indian tales, the coyote is a raven; in the Brothers Grimm he is the Big Bad Bear and he's not content with seduction of grandmother, he eats her too. (In earlier versions, Little Red Riding Hood is eaten too, hinting that cannibalism was just as much a feature of enlightened Europe as it was of the jungles bordering the

Congo and Amazon Rivers.) For years the coyote sneaks in and out of tents, having a marvelous time getting even with the tribe. None of the males in the tribe can figure why so many children are being born at the same time, curiously resembling each other (hooked nails, eager moustaches). During times of drought, famine, no buffalo, flooding, disease (small pox from the white Man), earthquakes, or tornadoes, coyote-man re-enters the tribe to take control. With his superior knowledge of nature, he knows where to find safety (Red Cloud, leading the Sioux into Canada) or sustenance. The scapegoat as hero and savior has come full circle and in this tale you can substitute Nelson Mandela, Moses, Christ, Geronimo, Mohammed, Black Elk, Mahatma Gandhi, Lumumba, etc. Of course there are all sorts of false coyote men, figures who lead their peoples out of one sort of bondage only to substitute another, far more severe than the first: Hitler, Castro, Mao Tse-Tung; in the more democratized countries, it has been the mob, substituting one technological tyranny with another, according to the latest fashion.

No better illustration of a modern coyote man is to be found than Malcolm X. You can read all about it in his *Autobiography*, but suffice to say he corrects the white man's version of history so that we realize what Kerouac knew before he began *On the Road* – that most of what we are told about the past is a lie. Now the slate is clean. We can begin afresh. New stories, new heroes. A whole new way of life with new allegiances more in tune with nature and our natural selves, and away from the dreary mechanized swamp of the moneylenders.

If you don't think Dean Moriarty was at the center of a modern revolution, take another look. None of the movements in music, politics, lifestyles, literature would have happened without him. He is directly responsible for Ken Kesey and The Merry Pranksters; the false propaganda surrounding him pushed millions of people away from money and power and toward personal freedom. If millions of young Americans were oriented toward a life of service and not a commitment to business, it was because their teachers and inspiring writers first sat at the feet of Dean Moriarty, took a look around the once-fabled Promised Land and found it not so wanting after all, its people neither lacking in generosity nor intelligence, just hungry for a little music and some inventive food that would give them a reason to put their loneliness, silly ambition, and suspicions in cold storage, and go out and have a little fun before the night closed in on them. Kerouac and Moriarty did all this and more.

Kerouac and his hero, Dean Moriarty, were merely saying what the British poet W.H. Auden had said a few years earlier, "Teach the free man how to praise." But you needed something worthwhile to praise. Auden spoke on behalf of W.B. Yeats; Kerouac speaks on behalf of his new knight, Moriarty. Miller, in discussing Kerouac in a letter to Lawrence Durrell, said he liked Kerouac because the latter had "that swing." The circle becomes complete when the father of jazz, Duke Ellington, says, "If you don't have that swing you don't have a thing."

a bibliographic note

Charles Bukowski wrote over 40 books encompassing stories, novels, and poetry. He had the reputation of a "wild man" for his depictions of drunks, whores, and crackpots that find their way to his Los Angeles apartments, but like most reputations, this one leaves out an important truth: Bukowski was liable to say anything at anytime.

In 1967, he first attracted a large following through his column, "Notes of a Dirty Old Man," written for the LA alternative *Open City*. His work has been translated into a dozen languages and he has the status of a rock star in Italy and Germany. A film, *Barfly*, was made in 1987 about an early part of his life.

Among the prose, my own favorites are *Ham on Rye*, *Factotum*, and *Post Office*; or among the poetry, I would suggest *Love Is a Dog From Hell* and *You Get So Alone at Times That It Just Makes Sense*. But all of Bukowski makes for reading you've never met before.

Books by **Irving Stettner** are hard to find, but try www.strokerpress.com as a starting point.

The novels and stories of **B. Traven** go in and out of print in various editions. Perhaps the most comprehensive body of his work in English is contained in the Hill and Wang hardcover series of some years ago of his "Jungle Novels," as well as other works. Edward Dee, Inc. (Qicaago, IL) also has reissued the works. Most public and university libraries have at least some of his books. Try to find them. Then read them.

Richard Yates' work includes *Eleven Kinds of Loneliness*, *Disturbing the Peace*, and *Revolutionary Road*. The latter was made into a movie three years ago.

Eduardo Galeano's writing includes *Open Veins of Latin America*, *Memory of Fire* – trilogy of the history of Latin America, *Book Of Embraces*, *Mirrors*, and many more.

Alexander Herzen's most notable work is *My Life & Past Thoughts*, the most lucid of histories of the failure of the revolutions of Europe in the 19th century.

Jack Kerouac's *On the Road* is part of the legacy of freedom. He also wrote *Dharma Bums*, and *The Subterraneans*.

ABOUT **PINTER & MARTIN**

Pinter & Martin is an independent book publisher based in London, with distribution throughout the world. We specialise in psychology, pregnancy, birth and parenting, fiction and yoga, and publish authors who challenge the status quo, such as Elliot Aronson, Grantly Dick-Read, Ina May Gaskin, Stanley Milgram, Guillermo O'Joyce, Michel Odent, Gabrielle Palmer, Stuart Sutherland and Frank Zappa.

For more information, visit www.pinterandmartin.com